COMPLETE WORKS:
THREE

This book is Volume Three of the Collected Works of Harold Pinter.

D0032227

Works by Harold Pinter published by Grove Press

Complete Works: One (The Birthday Party • *The Room* • *The Dumb Waiter* • *A Slight Ache* • *A Night Out* • "The Black and White" • "The Examination" • "Writing for the Theatre")

Complete Works: Two (The Caretaker • *The Dwarfs* [play] • *The Collection* • *The Lover* • *Night School* • *Trouble in the Works* • *The Black and White* • *Request Stop* • *Last to Go* • *Special Offer* • "Writing for Myself ")

Complete Works: Three (The Homecoming • *The Basement* • *Landscape* • *Silence* • *Night* • *That's Your Trouble* • *That's All* • *Applicant* • *Interview* • *Dialogue for Three* • *Tea Party* [play] • "Tea Party" [short story] • "Mac")

Complete Works: Four (Old Times • *No Man's Land* • *Betrayal* • *Monologue* • *Family Voices)*

PLAYS AND SCREENPLAYS
Ashes to Ashes
Betrayal
The Birthday Party and The Room
The Caretaker and The Dumb Waiter
Five Screenplays (The Servant • *The Pumpkin Eater* • *The Quiller Memorandum* • *Accident* • *The Go-Between)*
The Homecoming
Moonlight
Mountain Language
No Man's Land
Old Times
One for the Road
Other Places: Three Plays (A Kind of Alaska • *Victoria Station* • *Family Voices)*
Party Time and The New World Order

POETRY AND PROSE
Collected Poems and Prose
The Dwarfs: A Novel
100 Poems by 100 Poets (an anthology selected by Harold Pinter, Geoffrey Godbert, and Anthony Astbury)
99 Poems in Translation (an anthology selected by Harold Pinter, Geoffrey Godbert, and Anthony Astbury)
Various Voices

HAROLD PINTER

COMPLETE WORKS: THREE

THE HOMECOMING

TEA PARTY

THE BASEMENT

LANDSCAPE

SILENCE

REVUE SKETCHES:
Night
That's Your Trouble
That's All
Applicant
Interview
Dialogue for Three

With the memoir "Mac" and the short story "Tea Party"

GROVE PRESS
New York

Printed in the United States of America

Library of Congress Cataloging-in-Publication Data
Pinter, Harold 1930–
    Works. 1990]
    Complete works / Harold Pinter.
      p. cm.
    ISBN 0-8021-5049-7 (v.3)
    I. Title.
PR6066.I53   1990
822'.914—dc20   90-13933

Grove Press
841 Broadway
New York, NY 10003

03   10 9 8 7 6 5 4

Contents

Chronology   7

Mac   9

THE HOMECOMING   19

TEA PARTY   99

THE BASEMENT   149

LANDSCAPE   173

SILENCE   199

REVUE SKETCHES   221

   Night   223

   That's Your Trouble   227

   That's All   229

   Applicant   231

   Interview   235

   Dialogue for Three   239

Tea Party (short story)   241

Harold Pinter: A Chronology

Year of writing		First performance
1954–5	The Black and White	(short story)
1955	The Examination	(short story)
1957	The Room	May 15, 1957
1957	The Birthday Party	April 28, 1958
1957	The Dumb Waiter	January 21, 1960
1958	A Slight Ache	July 29, 1959
1958	The Hothouse	April 24, 1980
1959	Revue sketches—	
	Trouble in the Works;	
	The Black and White	July 15, 1959
	Request Stop; Last to Go;	
	Special Offer	September 23, 1959
	That's Your Trouble;	
	That's All; Applicant;	
	Interview;	
	Dialogue for Three	February–March 1964
1959	A Night Out	March 1, 1960
1959	The Caretaker	April 27, 1960
1960	Night School	July 21, 1960
1960	The Dwarfs	December 2, 1960
1961	The Collection	May 11, 1961
1962	The Lover	March 28, 1963
1963	Tea Party	(short story)
1964	Tea Party	March 25, 1965
1964	The Homecoming	June 3, 1965
1966	The Basement	February 28, 1967
1967	Landscape	April 25, 1968
1968	Silence	July 2, 1969
1969	Night	April 9, 1969
1970	Old Times	June 1, 1971
1972	Monologue	April 10, 1973
1974	No Man's Land	April 23, 1975
1978	Betrayal	November 15, 1978
1980	Family Voices	January 22, 1981
1982	Victoria Station	performed with *Family*
	A Kind of Alaska	*Voices* as a trilogy titled
		Other Places in 1982
1984	One for the Road	March 15, 1984
1988	Mountain Language	October 20, 1988

Mac

BIOGRAPHICAL NOTE

ANEW MCMASTER was born in County Monaghan on Christmas Eve 1894 and was 16 when he made his first stage appearance as 'The Aristocrat' in 'The Scarlet Pimpernel' with Fred Terry at the New Theatre, London. He died in Dublin on August 25th, 1962, a few days after appearing in the 'dream scene' from 'The Bells' at an Equity concert. His acting career had spanned half a century and his death was the end of an era. He was the last of the great actor-managers, unconnected with films and television.

From 1925 onwards he and his company played a repertoire of Shakespeare's plays across the world and the roles which made his reputation were Hamlet, Macbeth, Coriolanus, Petruchio, Richard III, Shylock and, above all, Othello. He occasionally played outside his company as when he took over from Fredric March to tour America in the Broadway production of O'Neill's 'Long Day's Journey into Night', but he was never long away from Shakespeare or Ireland. When asked why, he replied 'I suppose I'm a wanderer and I like playing in the theatre. It makes no difference to me if I'm on Broadway or in the smallest village hall in Ireland. The only thing that matters is that I am playing.'

I've been the toast of twelve continents and eight hemispheres!
Mac said from his hotel bed. I'll see none of my admirers before
noon. Marjorie, where are my teeth? His teeth were brought to
him. None before noon, he said, and looked out of the window.
If the clergy call say I am studying King Lear and am not to be
disturbed. How long have you been studying King Lear, Mac?
Since I was a boy. I can play the part. It's the lines I can't learn.
That's the problem. The part I can do. I think. What do you
think? Do you think I can do it? I wonder if I'm wise to want to
do it, or unwise? But I will do it. I'll do it next season. Don't
forget I was acclaimed for my performance in Paddy The Next
Best Thing. Never forget that. Should I take Othello to the Embassy, Swiss Cottage? Did you know Godfrey Tearle left out the
fit? He didn't do the fit. I'm older than Godfrey Tearle. But I
do the fit. Don't I? At least I don't leave it out. What's your
advice? Should I take Othello to the Embassy, Swiss Cottage?
Look out the window at this town. What a stinking diseased
abandoned Godforgotten bog. What am I playing tonight,
Marjorie? The Taming of the Shrew? But you see one thing the
Irish peasantry really appreciate is style, grace and wit. You have
a lovely company, someone said to me the other day, a lovely
company, all the boys is like girls. Joe, are the posters up? Will
we pack out? I was just driving into this town and I had to brake
at a dung heap. A cow looked in through the window. No auto-
graphs today, I said. Let's have a drop of whiskey, for Jesus' sake.

Pat Magee phoned me from Ireland to tell me Mac was dead. I
decided to go to the funeral. At London Airport the plane was
very late leaving. I hadn't been in Ireland for ten years. The taxi

raced through Dublin. We passed the Sinn Fein Hall, where we used to rehearse five plays in two weeks. But I knew I was too late for the funeral. The cemetery was empty. I saw no one I knew. I didn't know Mrs. Mac's address. I knew no one any more in Dublin. I couldn't find Mac's grave.

I toured Ireland with Mac for about two years in the early 1950's. He advertised in 'The Stage' for actors for a Shakespearian tour of the country. I sent him a photograph and went to see him in a flat near Willesden Junction. At the time Willesden Junction seemed to me as likely a place as any to meet a manager from whom you might get work. But after I knew Mac our first meeting place became more difficult to accept or understand. I still wonder what he was doing interviewing actors at Willesden Junction. But I never asked him. He offered me six pounds a week, said I could get digs for twenty-five shillings at the most, told me how cheap cigarettes were and that I could play Horatio, Bassanio and Cassio. It was my first job proper on the stage.

Those two? It must be like two skeletons copulating on a bed of corrugated iron. (The actor and actress Mac was talking about were very thin.) He undercuts me, he said, he keeps coming in under me. I'm the one who should come under. I'm playing Hamlet. But how can I play Hamlet if he keeps coming under me all the time? The more under I go the more under he goes. Nobody in the audience can hear a word. The bugger wants to play Hamlet himself, that's what it is. But he bloodywell won't while I'm alive. When I die I hope I die quickly. I couldn't face months of bedpans. Sheer hell. Days and months of bedpans. Do you think we'll go to heaven? I mean me. Do you think I'll go to heaven? You never saw me play the Cardinal. My cloak was superb, the length of the stage, crimson. I had six boys from the village to carry it. They used to kiss my ring every night before we made our entrance. When I made my tour of Australia and the southern hemisphere we were the guests of honour at a city banquet. The Mayor stood up. He said: We are honoured today to welcome to our city one of the most famous actors in the world, an actor who has given tremendous pleasure to people all over the world, to worldwide acclaim. It is my great privilege to introduce to you – Andrew MacPherson!

Joe Nolan, the business manager, came in one day and said: Mac, all the cinemas in Limerick are on strike. What shall I do? Book Limerick! Mac said. At once! We'll open on Monday. There was no theatre in the town. We opened on the Monday in a two thousand seater cinema, with Othello. There was no stage and no wingspace. It was St Patrick's night. The curtain was supposed to rise at nine o'clock. But the house wasn't full until eleven thirty, so the play didn't begin until then. It was well past two in the morning before the curtain came down. Everyone of the two thousand people in the audience was drunk. Apart from that, they weren't accustomed to Shakespeare. For the first half of the play, up to 'I am your own for ever', we could not hear ourselves speak, could not hear our cues. The cast was alarmed. We expected the audience on stage at any moment. We kept our hands on our swords. I was playing Iago at the time. I came offstage with Mac at the interval and gasped. Don't worry, Mac said, don't worry. After the interval he began to move. When he walked onto the stage for the 'Naked in bed, Iago, and not mean harm' scene (his great body hunched, his voice low with grit), they silenced. He tore into the fit. He made the play his and the place his. By the time he had reached 'It is the very error of the moon; She comes more near the earth than she was wont, And makes men mad.', (the word 'mad' suddenly cauterized, ugly, shocking) the audience was quite still. And sober. I congratulated Mac. Not bad, he said, was it? Not bad. Godfrey Tearle never did the fit, you know.

Mac gave about half a dozen magnificent performances of Othello while I was with him. Even when, on the other occasions, he con-

served his energies in the role, he always gave the patrons their
moneysworth. At his best his was the finest Othello I have seen.
His age was always a mystery, but I would think he was in his
sixties at the time. Sometimes, late at night, after the show, he
looked very old. But on stage in Othello he stood, well over six
foot, naked to the waist, his gestures complete, final, nothing
jagged, his movement of the utmost fluidity and yet of the utmost
precision: stood there, dead in the centre of the role, and the
great sweeping symphonic playing would begin, the rare tension
and release within him, the arrest, the swoop, the savagery, the
majesty and repose. His voice was unique: in my experience of an
unequalled range. A bass of extraordinary echo, resonance and
gut, and remarkable sweep up into tenor, when the note would hit
the back of the gallery and come straight back, a brilliant, stunning
sound. I remember his delivery of this line: 'Methinks (bass) it
should be now a huge (bass) eclipse (tenor) Of sun and moon
(baritone) and that th'affrighted globe (bass) Should yawn (very
deep, the abyss) at alteration.' We all watched him from the
wings.

He was capable, of course, of many indifferent and offhand performances. On these occasions an edgy depression and fatigue
hung over him. He would gabble his way through the part, his
movement fussed, his voice acting outside him, the man himself detached from its acrobatics. At such times his eyes would
fix upon the other actors, appraising them coldly, emanating
a grim dissatisfaction with himself and his company. Afterwards, over a drink, he would confide: I was bad tonight,
wasn't I, really awful, but the damn cast was even worse. What
a lot.

He was never a good Hamlet and for some reason or other rarely
bothered to play Macbeth. He was obsessed with the lighting in
Macbeth and more often than not spent half his time on stage
glaring at the spot bar. Yet there was plenty of Macbeth in him. I

believe his dislike of the play was so intense he couldn't bring himself to play it.

It was consistent with him that after many months of coasting through Shylock he suddenly lashed fullfired into the role at an obscure matinee in a onehorse village; a frightening performance. Afterwards he said to me: What did I do? Did you notice? I did something different. What did you think of it? What was it I did? He never did it again. Not quite like that. Who saw it?

In the trial scene in The Merchant of Venice one night I said to him (as Bassanio) instead of 'For thy three thousand ducats here is six', quite involuntarily, 'For thy three thousand *buckets* here is six'. He replied quietly and with emphasis: 'If every *bucket* in six thousand *buckets* were in six parts, and every part a *bucket* I would not draw them – I would have my bond'. I could not continue. The other members of the court scene and I turned upstage. Some walked into the wings. But Mac stood, remorseless, grave, like an eagle, waiting for my reply.

Sometimes after a matinee of Macbeth and an evening of Othello we all stayed on stage, he'd get someone to put on a record of Faust, disappear behind a curtain, reappear in a long golden wig, without his teeth, mime Marguerite weaving, mime Faust and Mephistopheles, deliver at full tilt the aria from Verdi's Othello 'Era La Notte e Cassio Dormia', while the caretaker swept the dust up, and then in a bar talk for hours of Sarah and Mrs. Pat Campbell, with relish, malice and devotion. I think he would still be talking about them now, if he wasn't dead, because they did something he knew about.

In order to present Oedipus the company had to recruit extras from the town or village we were in. One night in Dundalk Mac was building up to his blind climax when one of the extras had an epileptic fit on stage and collapsed. He was dragged to the wings where various women attended to him. The sounds of their ministrations seeped onto the stage. Mac stopped, turned to the wings and shouted: 'For God's sake, can't you see I'm trying to act!'

His concentration was always complete in Oedipus. He was at his best in the part. He acted with acute 'underness' and tenacity. And he never used his vocal powers to better or truer effect. He acted along the spine of the role and never deviated from it. As in his two other great roles, Othello and Lear, he understood and expressed totally the final tender clarity which is under the storm, the blindness, the anguish. For me his acting at these times embodied the idea of Yeats' line: 'They know that Hamlet and Lear are gay, Gaiety transfiguring all that dread'. Mac entered into this tragic gaiety naturally and inevitably.

He did Lear eventually. First performance somewhere in County Clare, Ennis, I think. Knew most of the lines. *Was* the old man, tetchy, appalled, feverish. Wanted the storm louder. All of us banged the thundersheets. No, they can still hear me. Hit it, hit it. He got above the noise. I played Edgar in Lear only a few times with him before I left the company. At the centre of his performance was a terrible loss, desolation, silence. He didn't think about doing it, he just got there. He did it and got there.

His wife, Marjorie, was his structure and support. She organised the tours, supervised all business arrangements, sat in the box office, kept the cast in order, ran the wardrobe, sewed, looked after Mac, was his dresser, gave him his whiskey. She was tough, critical, cultivated, devoted. Her spirit and belief constituted the backbone of the company. There would have been no company without her.

Ireland wasn't golden always, but it was golden sometimes and in 1950 it was, all in all, a golden age for me and for others.

The people came down to see him. Mac travelled by car, and
sometimes some of us did too. But other times we went on the
lorry with the flats and props, and going into Bandon or Clough-
jordan would find the town empty, asleep, men sitting upright in
dark bars, cowpads, mud, smell of peat, wood, old clothes. We'd
find digs; wash basin and jug, tea, black pudding, and off to the
hall, set up a stage on trestle tables, a few rostra, a few drapes,
costumes out of the hampers, set up shop, and at night play, not
always but mostly, to a packed house (where had they come
from?); people who listened, and who waited to see him, having
seen him before, and been brought up on him.

Mac wasn't any kind of dreamer. He was remote from the Celtic
Twilight. He kept a close eye on the box office receipts. He was
sharp about money, was as depressed as anyone else when business
was bad. Where there was any kind of company disagreement he
proved elusive. He distanced himself easily from unwelcome
problems. Mrs Mac dealt with those. Mac was never 'a darling
actor of the old school'. He was a working man. He respected his
occupation and never stopped learning about it, from himself and
from others.

For those who cared for him and admired him there must remain
one great regret; that for reasons I do not understand, he last
played in England, at Stratford, in 1933. The loser was the
English theatre.

Mac wasn't 'childlike' in temperament, as some have said. He
was evasive, proud, affectionate, mischievous, shrewd, merry,
cynical, sad, and could be callous. But he was never sour or self-
pitying. His life was the stage. Life with a big L came a bad
second. He had no patience with what he considered a world of
petty sufferings, however important they might seem to the
bearer. He was completely unsentimental. Gossip delighted him,
and particularly sexual gossip. He moved with great flexibility

and amusement through Catholic Ireland, greatly attracted by the ritual of the Church. He loved to speak of the mummy of the Blessed Oliver Plunkett in Drogheda 'with a lovely amber spot on its face'. He mixed freely with priests and nuns, went to Mass, sometimes, but despised the religious atrophy, rigidity and complacency with which he was confronted. He mixed with the priests partly because he enjoyed their company, partly because his livelihood depended upon them. He was a realist. But he possessed a true liberality of spirit. He was humble. He was a devout anti-puritan. He was a very great piss-taker. He was a great actor and we who worked with him were the luckiest people in the world and loved him.

The Homecoming

THE HOMECOMING was first presented by the Royal Shakespeare Company at the Aldwych Theatre on 3 June, 1965, with the following cast:

MAX, *a man of seventy*	Paul Rogers
LENNY, *a man in his early thirties*	Ian Holm
SAM, *a man of sixty-three*	John Normington
JOEY, *a man in his middle twenties*	Terence Rigby
TEDDY, *a man in his middle thirties*	Michael Bryant
RUTH, *a woman in her early thirties*	Vivien Merchant

Directed by Peter Hall

The play was presented by the Royal Shakespeare Company and Alexander H. Cohen at the Music Box Theatre, New York, on 5 January, 1967 with one change in the cast: the part of Teddy was played by Michael Craig.

SUMMER

An old house in North London.
A large room, extending the width of the stage.
The back wall, which contained the door, has been removed.
A square arch shape remains. Beyond it, the hall. In the hall a
staircase, ascending up left, well in view. The front door up right.
A coatstand, hooks, etc.

In the room a window, right. Odd tables, chairs. Two large
armchairs. A large sofa, left. Against the right wall a large sideboard, the upper half of which contains a mirror. Up left, a
radiogram.

Act One

Evening.

LENNY is sitting on the sofa with a newspaper, a pencil in his hand. He wears a dark suit. He makes occasional marks on the back page.

MAX comes in, from the direction of the kitchen. He goes to sideboard, opens top drawer, rummages in it, closes it.

He wears an old cardigan and a cap, and carries a stick.

He walks downstage, stands, looks about the room.

MAX. What have you done with the scissors?

Pause.

I said I'm looking for the scissors. What have you done with them?

Pause.

Did you hear me? I want to cut something out of the paper.

LENNY. I'm reading the paper.

MAX. Not that paper. I haven't even read that paper. I'm talking about last Sunday's paper. I was just having a look at it in the kitchen.

Pause.

Do you hear what I'm saying? I'm talking to you! Where's the scissors?

LENNY (*looking uo, quietly*). Why don't you shut up, you daft prat?

MAX lifts his stick and points it at him.

MAX. Don't you talk to me like that. I'm warning you.

He sits in large armchair.

There's an advertisement in the paper about flannel vests. Cut price. Navy surplus. I could do with a few of them.

Pause.

I think I'll have a fag. Give me a fag.

Pause.

I just asked you to give me a cigarette.

Pause.

Look what I'm lumbered with.

He takes a crumpled cigarette from his pocket.

I'm getting old, my word of honour.

He lights it.

You think I wasn't a tearaway? I could have taken care of you, twice over. I'm still strong. You ask your Uncle Sam what I was. But at the same time I always had a kind heart. Always.

Pause.

I used to knock about with a man called MacGregor. I called him Mac. You remember Mac? Eh?

Pause.

Huhh! We were two of the worst hated men in the West End of London. I tell you, I still got the scars. We'd walk into a place, the whole room'd stand up, they'd make way to let us pass. You never heard such silence. Mind you, he was a big man, he was over six foot tall. His family were all MacGregors, they came all the way from Aberdeen, but he was the only one they called Mac.

Pause.

He was very fond of your mother, Mac was. Very fond. He always had a good word for her.

Pause.

Mind you, she wasn't such a bad woman. Even though it made me sick just to look at her rotten stinking face, she wasn't such a bad bitch. I gave her the best bleeding years of my life, anyway.

LENNY. Plug it, will you, you stupid sod, I'm trying to read the paper.

MAX. Listen! I'll chop your spine off, you talk to me like that! You understand? Talking to your lousy filthy father like that!

LENNY. You know what, you're getting demented.

Pause.

What do you think of Second Wind for the three-thirty?

MAX. Where?

LENNY. Sandown Park.

MAX. Don't stand a chance.

LENNY. Sure he does.

MAX. Not a chance.

LENNY. He's the winner.

LENNY *ticks the paper.*

MAX. He talks to me about horses.

Pause.

I used to live on the course. One of the loves of my life. Epsom? I knew it like the back of my hand. I was one of the best-known faces down at the paddock. What a marvellous open-air life.

Pause.

He talks to me about horses. You only read their names in the papers. But I've stroked their manes, I've held them, I've calmed them down before a big race. I was the one they used to call for. Max, they'd say, there's a horse here, he's highly strung, you're the only man on the course who can calm him. It was true. I had a . . . I had an instinctive understanding of animals. I should have been a trainer. Many times I was offered the job – you know, a proper post, by the Duke of . . . I forget his name . . . one of the Dukes. But I had family obligations, my family needed me at home.

Pause.

The times I've watched those animals thundering past the post. What an experience. Mind you, I didn't lose, I made a few bob out of it, and you know why? Because I always had the smell of a good horse. I could smell him. And not only the colts but the fillies. Because the fillies are more highly strung than the colts, they're more unreliable, did you know that? No, what do you know? Nothing. But I was always able to tell a good filly by one particular trick. I'd look her in the eye. You see? I'd stand in front of her and look her straight in the eye, it was a kind of hypnotism, and by the look deep down in her eye I could tell whether she was a stayer or not. It was a gift. I had a gift.

Pause.

And he talks to me about horses.
LENNY. Dad, do you mind if I change the subject?

Pause.

I want to ask you something. The dinner we had before, what was the name of it? What do you call it?

Pause.

Why don't you buy a dog? You're a dog cook. Honest. You
think you're cooking for a lot of dogs.

MAX. If you don't like it get out.

LENNY. I am going out. I'm going out to buy myself a proper
dinner.

MAX. Well, get out! What are you waiting for?

LENNY *looks at him.*

LENNY. What did you say?

MAX. I said shove off out of it, that's what I said.

LENNY. You'll go before me, Dad, if you talk to me in that tone
of voice.

MAX. Will I, you bitch?

MAX *grips his stick.*

LENNY. Oh, Daddy, you're not going to use your stick on me,
are you? Eh? Don't use your stick on me Daddy. No,
please. It wasn't my fault, it was one of the others. I haven't
done anything wrong, Dad, honest. Don't clout me with that
stick, Dad.

Silence.

MAX *sits hunched.* LENNY *reads the paper.*

SAM *comes in the front door. He wears a chauffeur's uniform.
He hangs his hat on a hook in the hall and comes into the
room. He goes to a chair, sits in it and sighs.*

Hullo, Uncle Sam.

SAM. Hullo.

LENNY. How are you, Uncle?

SAM. Not bad. A bit tired.

LENNY. Tired? I bet you're tired. Where you been?

SAM. I've been to London Airport.

LENNY. All the way up to London Airport? What, right up the
M4?

SAM. Yes, all the way up there.

LENNY. Tch, tch, tch. Well, I think you're entitled to be tired, Uncle.

SAM. Well, it's the drivers.

LENNY. I know. That's what I'm talking about. I'm talking about the drivers.

SAM. Knocks you out.

Pause.

MAX. I'm here, too, you know.

SAM looks at him.

I said I'm here, too. I'm sitting here.

SAM. I know you're here.

Pause.

SAM. I took a Yankee out there today . . . to the Airport.

LENNY. Oh, a Yankee, was it?

SAM. Yes, I been with him all day. Picked him up at the Savoy at half past twelve, took him to the Caprice for his lunch. After lunch I picked him up again, took him down to a house in Eaton Square – he had to pay a visit to a friend there – and then round about tea-time I took him right the way out to the Airport.

LENNY. Had to catch a plane there, did he?

SAM. Yes. Look what he gave me. He gave me a box of cigars.

SAM takes a box of cigars from his pocket.

MAX. Come here. Let's have a look at them.

SAM shows MAX the cigars. MAX takes one from the box, pinches it and sniffs it.

It's a fair cigar.

SAM. Want to try one?

MAX and SAM light cigars.

You know what he said to me? He told me I was the best
chauffeur he'd ever had. The best one.

MAX. From what point of view?

SAM. Eh?

MAX. From what point of view?

LENNY. From the point of view of his driving, Dad, and his
general sense of courtesy, I should say.

MAX. Thought you were a good driver, did he, Sam? Well,
he gave you a first-class cigar.

SAM. Yes, he thought I was the best he'd ever had. They all
say that, you know. They won't have anyone else, they only
ask for me. They say I'm the best chauffeur in the firm.

LENNY. I bet the other drivers tend to get jealous, don't they,
Uncle?

SAM. They do get jealous. They get very jealous.

MAX. Why?

Pause.

SAM. I just told you.

MAX. No, I just can't get it clear, Sam. Why do the other
drivers get jealous?

SAM. Because (a) I'm the best driver, and because . . . (b)
I don't take liberties.

Pause.

I don't press myself on people, you see. These big business-
men, men of affairs, they don't want the driver jawing all
the time, they like to sit in the back, have a bit of peace and
quiet. After all, they're sitting in a Humber Super Snipe,
they can afford to relax. At the same time, though, this is
what really makes me special . . . I do know how to pass
the time of day when required.

Pause.

For instance, I told this man today I was in the second world war. Not the first. I told him I was too young for the first. But I told him I fought in the second.

Pause.

So did he, it turned out.

LENNY *stands, goes to the mirror and straightens his tie.*

LENNY. He was probably a colonel, or something, in the American Air Force.

SAM. Yes.

LENNY. Probably a navigator, or something like that, in a Flying Fortress. Now he's most likely a high executive in a worldwide group of aeronautical engineers.

SAM. Yes.

LENNY. Yes, I know the kind of man you're talking about.

LENNY *goes out, turning to his right.*

SAM. After all, I'm experienced. I was driving a dust cart at the age of nineteen. Then I was in long-distance haulage. I had ten years as a taxi-driver and I've had five as a private chauffeur.

MAX. It's funny you never got married, isn't it? A man with all your gifts.

Pause.

Isn't it? A man like you?

SAM. There's still time.

MAX. Is there?

Pause.

SAM. You'd be surprised.

MAX. What you been doing, banging away at your lady customers, have you?

SAM. Not me.

MAX. In the back of the Snipe? Been having a few crafty reefs in a layby, have you?

SAM. Not me.

MAX. On the back seat? What about the armrest, was it up or down?

SAM. I've never done that kind of thing in my car.

MAX. Above all that kind of thing, are you, Sam?

SAM. Too true.

MAX. Above having a good bang on the back seat, are you?

SAM. Yes, I leave that to others.

MAX. You leave it to others? What others? You paralysed prat!

SAM. I don't mess up my car! Or my . . . my boss's car! Like other people.

MAX. Other people? What other people?

Pause.

What other people?

Pause.

SAM. Other people.

Pause.

MAX. When you find the right girl, Sam, let your family know, don't forget, we'll give you a number one send-off, I promise you. You can bring her to live here, she can keep us all happy. We'd take it in turns to give her a walk round the park.

SAM. I wouldn't bring her here.

MAX. Sam, it's your decision. You're welcome to bring your bride here, to the place where you live, or on the other hand you can take a suite at the Dorchester. It's entirely up to you.

SAM. I haven't got a bride.

> SAM *stands, goes to the sideboard, takes an apple from the bowl, bites into it.*

Getting a bit peckish.

He looks out of the window.

Never get a bride like you had, anyway. Nothing like your bride . . . going about these days. Like Jessie.

Pause.

After all, I escorted her once or twice, didn't I? Drove her round once or twice in my cab. She was a charming woman.

Pause.

All the same, she was your wife. But still . . . they were some of the most delightful evenings I've ever had. Used to just drive her about. It was my pleasure.

MAX (*softly, closing his eyes*). Christ.

SAM. I used to pull up at a stall and buy her a cup of coffee. She was a very nice companion to be with.

Silence.
JOEY *comes in the front door. He walks into the room, takes his jacket off, throws it on a chair and stands.*
Silence.

JOEY. Feel a bit hungry.

SAM. Me, too.

MAX. Who do you think I am, your mother? Eh? Honest. They walk in here every time of the day and night like bloody animals. Go and find yourself a mother.

LENNY *walks into the room, stands.*

JOEY. I've been training down at the gym.

SAM. Yes, the boy's been working all day and training all night.

MAX. What do you want, you bitch? You spend all the day sitting on your arse at London Airport, buy yourself a jamroll. You expect me to sit here waiting to rush into the kitchen the moment you step in the door? You've been living sixty-three years, why don't you learn to cook?

SAM. I can cook.

MAX. Well, go and cook!

Pause.

LENNY. What the boys want, Dad, is your own special brand
of cooking, Dad. That's what the boys look forward to. The
special understanding of food, you know, that you've got.

MAX. Stop calling me Dad. Just stop all that calling me Dad,
do you understand?

LENNY. But I'm your son. You used to tuck me up in bed every
night. He tucked you up, too, didn't he, Joey?

Pause.

He used to like tucking up his sons.

LENNY *turns and goes towards the front door.*

MAX. Lenny.

LENNY (*turning*). What?

MAX. I'll give you a proper tuck up one of these nights, son
You mark my word.

They look at each other.
LENNY *opens the front door and goes out.*
Silence.

JOEY. I've been training with Bobby Dodd.

Pause.

And I had a good go at the bag as well.

Pause.

I wasn't in bad trim.

MAX. Boxing's a gentleman's game.

Pause.

I'll tell you what you've got to do. What you've got to do is
you've got to learn how to defend yourself, and you've got
to learn how to attack. That's your only trouble as a boxer.
You don't know how to defend yourself, and you don't know
how to attack.

Pause.

Once you've mastered those arts you can go straight to the top.

Pause.

JOEY. I've got a pretty good idea . . . of how to do that.

JOEY looks round for his jacket, picks it up, goes out of the room and up the stairs.
Pause.

MAX. Sam . . . why don't you go, too, eh? Why don't you just go upstairs? Leave me quiet. Leave me alone.

SAM. I want to make something clear about Jessie, Max. I want to. I do. When I took her out in the cab, round the town, I was taking care of her, for you. I was looking after her for you, when you were busy, wasn't I? I was showing her the West End.

Pause.

You wouldn't have trusted any of your other brothers. You wouldn't have trusted Mac, would you? But you trusted me. I want to remind you.

Pause.

Old Mac died a few years ago, didn't he? Isn't he dead?

Pause.

He was a lousy stinking rotten loudmouth. A bastard uncouth sodding runt. Mind you, he was a good friend of yours.

Pause.

MAX. Eh, Sam . . .
SAM. What?
MAX. Why do I keep you here? You're just an old grub.

SAM. Am I?

MAX. You're a maggot.

SAM. Oh yes?

MAX. As soon as you stop paying your way here, I mean when
you're too old to pay your way, you know what I'm going to
do? I'm going to give you the boot.

SAM. You are, eh?

MAX. Sure. I mean, bring in the money and I'll put up with
you. But when the firm gets rid of you – you can flake off.

SAM. This is my house as well, you know. This was our
mother's house.

MAX. One lot after the other. One mess after the other.

SAM. Our father's house.

MAX. Look what I'm lumbered with. One cast-iron bunch of
crap after another. One flow of stinking pus after another.

Pause.

Our father! I remember him. Don't worry. You kid yourself. He used to come over to me and look down at me. My
old man did. He'd bend right over me, then he'd pick me up.
I was only that big. Then he'd dandle me. Give me the
bottle. Wipe me clean. Give me a smile. Pat me on the bum.
Pass me around, pass me from hand to hand. Toss me up
in the air. Catch me coming down. I remember my father.

BLACKOUT.
LIGHTS UP.
Night.
TEDDY *and* RUTH *stand at the threshold of the room.*
*They are both well dressed in light summer suits and light
raincoats.*
Two suitcases are by their side.
They look at the room. TEDDY *tosses the key in his hand,
smiles.*

TEDDY. Well, the key worked.

Pause.

They haven't changed the lock.

Pause.

RUTH. No one's here.
TEDDY (*looking up*). They're asleep.

Pause.

RUTH. Can I sit down?
TEDDY. Of course.
RUTH. I'm tired.

Pause.

TEDDY. Then sit down.

She does not move.

That's my father's chair.
RUTH. That one?
TEDDY (*smiling*). Yes, that's it. Shall I go up and see if my room's still there?
RUTH. It can't have moved.
TEDDY. No, I mean if my bed's still there.
RUTH. Someone might be in it.
TEDDY. No. They've got their own beds.

Pause.

RUTH. Shouldn't you wake someone up? Tell them you're here?
TEDDY. Not at this time of night. It's too late.

Pause.

Shall I go up?

He goes into the hall, looks up the stairs, comes back.

Why don't you sit down?

Pause.

I'll just go up . . . have a look.

He goes up the stairs, stealthily.
RUTH *stands, then slowly walks across the room.*
TEDDY *returns.*

It's still there. My room. Empty. The bed's there. What are you doing?

She looks at him.

Blankets, no sheets. I'll find some sheets. I could hear snores. Really. They're all still here, I think. They're all snoring up there. Are you cold?

RUTH. No.

TEDDY. I'll make something to drink, if you like. Something hot.

RUTH. No, I don't want anything.

TEDDY *walks about.*

TEDDY. What do you think of the room? Big, isn't it? It's a big house. I mean, it's a fine room, don't you think? Actually there was a wall, across there . . . with a door. We knocked it down . . . years ago . . . to make an open living area. The structure wasn't affected, you see. My mother was dead.

RUTH *sits.*

Tired?

RUTH. Just a little.

TEDDY. We can go to bed if you like. No point in waking anyone up now. Just go to bed. See them all in the morning . . . see my father in the morning. . . .

Pause.

RUTH. Do you want to stay?

TEDDY. Stay?

Pause.

We've come to stay. We're bound to stay . . . for a few days.

RUTH. I think . . . the children . . . might be missing us.

TEDDY. Don't be silly.

RUTH. They might.

TEDDY. Look, we'll be back in a few days, won't we?

He walks about the room.

Nothing's changed. Still the same.

Pause.

Still, he'll get a surprise in the morning, won't he? The old man. I think you'll like him very much. Honestly. He's a . . . well, he's old, of course. Getting on.

Pause.

I was born here, do you realize that?

RUTH. I know.

Pause.

TEDDY. Why don't you go to bed? I'll find some sheets. I feel . . . wide awake, isn't it odd? I think I'll stay up for a bit. Are you tired?

RUTH. No.

TEDDY. Go to bed. I'll show you the room.

RUTH. No, I don't want to.

TEDDY. You'll be perfectly all right up there without me. Really you will. I mean, I won't be long. Look, it's just up there. It's the first door on the landing. The bathroom's right next door. You . . . need some rest, you know.

Pause.

I just want to . . . walk about for a few minutes. Do you
mind?

RUTH. Of course I don't.

TEDDY. Well . . . Shall I show you the room?

RUTH. No, I'm happy at the moment.

TEDDY. You don't have to go to bed. I'm not saying you have
to. I mean, you can stay up with me. Perhaps I'll make a
cup of tea or something. The only thing is we don't want to
make too much noise, we don't want to wake anyone up.

RUTH. I'm not making any noise.

TEDDY. I know you're not.

He goes to her.

(*Gently.*) Look, it's all right, really. I'm here. I mean . . .
I'm with you. There's no need to be nervous. Are you
nervous?

RUTH. No.

TEDDY. There's no need to be.

Pause.

They're very warm people, really. Very warm. They're my
family. They're not ogres.

Pause.

Well, perhaps we should go to bed. After all, we have to
be up early, see Dad. Wouldn't be quite right if he found us
in bed, I think. (*He chuckles.*) Have to be up before six,
come down, say hullo.

Pause.

RUTH. I think I'll have a breath of air.

TEDDY. Air?

Pause.

What do you mean?

RUTH (*standing*). Just a stroll.

TEDDY. At this time of night? But we've . . . only just got here. We've got to go to bed.

RUTH. I just feel like some air.

TEDDY. But I'm going to bed.

RUTH. That's all right.

TEDDY. But what am I going to do?

    Pause.

The last thing I want is a breath of air. Why do you want a breath of air?

RUTH. I just do.

TEDDY. But it's late.

RUTH. I won't go far. I'll come back.

    Pause.

TEDDY. I'll wait up for you.

RUTH. Why?

TEDDY. I'm not going to bed without you.

RUTH. Can I have the key?

    He gives it to her.

Why don't you go to bed?

    He puts his arms on her shoulders and kisses her.
    They look at each other, briefly. She smiles.

I won't be long.

    She goes out of the front door.
    TEDDY *goes to the window, peers out after her, half turns from the window, stands, suddenly chews his knuckles.*
    LENNY *walks into the room from* U.L. *He stands. He wears pyjamas and dressing-gown. He watches* TEDDY.
    TEDDY *turns and sees him.*
    Silence.

TEDDY. Hullo, Lenny.

LENNY. Hullo, Teddy.

Pause.

TEDDY. I didn't hear you come down the stairs.

LENNY. I didn't.

Pause.

I sleep down here now. Next door. I've got a kind of study, workroom cum bedroom next door now, you see.

TEDDY. Oh. Did I . . . wake you up?

LENNY. No. I just had an early night tonight. You know how it is. Can't sleep. Keep waking up.

Pause

TEDDY. How are you?

LENNY. Well, just sleeping a bit restlessly, that's all. Tonight, anyway.

TEDDY. Bad dreams?

LENNY. No, I wouldn't say I was dreaming. It's not exactly a dream. It's just that something keeps waking me up. Some kind of tick.

TEDDY. A tick?

LENNY. Yes.

TEDDY. Well, what is it?

LENNY. I don't know.

Pause.

TEDDY. Have you got a clock in your room?

LENNY. Yes.

TEDDY. Well, maybe it's the clock.

LENNY. Yes, could be, I suppose.

Pause.

Well, if it's the clock I'd better do something about it, Stifle it in some way, or something.

Pause.

TEDDY. I've . . . just come back for a few days
LENNY. Oh yes? Have you?

Pause.

TEDDY. How's the old man?
LENNY. He's in the pink.

Pause.

TEDDY. I've been keeping well.
LENNY. Oh, have you?

Pause.

Staying the night then, are you?
TEDDY. Yes.
LENNY. Well, you can sleep in your old room.
TEDDY. Yes, I've been up.
LENNY. Yes, you can sleep there.

LENNY *yawns.*

Oh well.
TEDDY. I'm going to bed.
LENNY. Are you?
TEDDY. Yes, I'll get some sleep.
LENNY. Yes I'm going to bed, too.

TEDDY *picks up the cases.*

I'll give you a hand.
TEDDY. No, they're not heavy.

TEDDY *goes into the hall with the cases.*
LENNY *turns out the light in the room.*
The light in the hall remains on.
LENNY *follows into the hall.*

LENNY. Nothing you want?

TEDDY. Mmmm?

LENNY. Nothing you might want, for the night? Glass of water, anything like that?

TEDDY. Any sheets anywhere?

LENNY. In the sideboard in your room.

TEDDY. Oh, good.

LENNY. Friends of mine occasionally stay there, you know, in your room, when they're passing through this part of the world.

> LENNY *turns out the hall light and turns on the first landing light.*
> TEDDY *begins to walk up the stairs.*

TEDDY. Well, I'll see you at breakfast, then.

LENNY. Yes, that's it. Ta-ta.

> TEDDY *goes upstairs.*
> LENNY *goes off* L.
> *Silence.*
> *The landing light goes out.*
> *Slight night light in the hall and room.*
> LENNY *comes back into the room, goes to the window and looks out.*
> *He leaves the window and turns on a lamp.*
> *He is holding a small clock.*
> *He sits, places the clock in front of him, lights a cigarette and sits.*
> RUTH *comes in the front door.*
> *She stands still.* LENNY *turns his head, smiles. She walks slowly into the room.*

LENNY. Good evening.

RUTH. Morning, I think.

LENNY. You're right there.

> *Pause.*

My name's Lenny. What's yours?

RUTH. Ruth.

She sits, puts her coat collar around her.

LENNY. Cold?

RUTH. No.

LENNY. It's been a wonderful summer, hasn't it? Remarkable.

Pause.

Would you like something? Refreshment of some kind? An aperitif, anything like that?

RUTH. No, thanks.

LENNY. I'm glad you said that. We haven't got a drink in the house. Mind you, I'd soon get some in, if we had a party or something like that. Some kind of celebration . . . you know.

Pause.

You must be connected with my brother in some way. The one who's been abroad.

RUTH. I'm his wife.

LENNY. Eh listen, I wonder if you can advise me. I've been having a bit of a rough time with this clock. The tick's been keeping me up. The trouble is I'm not all that convinced it was the clock. I mean there are lots of things which tick in the night, don't you find that? All sorts of objects, which, in the day, you wouldn't call anything else but commonplace. They give you no trouble. But in the night any given one of a number of them is liable to start letting out a bit of a tick. Whereas you look at these objects in the day and they're just commonplace. They're as quiet as mice during the daytime. So . . . all things being equal . . . this question of me saying it was the clock that woke me up, well, that could very easily prove something of a false hypothesis.

He goes to the sideboard, pours from a jug into a glass, takes the glass to RUTH.

Here you are. I bet you could do with this.

RUTH. What is it?

LENNY. Water.

She takes it, sips, places the glass on a small table by her chair.

LENNY *watches her.*

Isn't it funny? I've got my pyjamas on and you're fully dressed.

He goes to the sideboard and pours another glass of water.

Mind if I have one? Yes, it's funny seeing my old brother again after all these years. It's just the sort of tonic my Dad needs, you know. He'll be chuffed to his bollocks in the morning, when he sees his eldest son. I was surprised myself when I saw Teddy, you know. Old Ted. I thought he was in America.

RUTH. We're on a visit to Europe.

LENNY. What, both of you?

RUTH. Yes.

LENNY. What, you sort of live with him over there, do you?

RUTH. We're married.

LENNY. On a visit to Europe, eh? Seen much of it?

RUTH. We've just come from Italy.

LENNY. Oh, you went to Italy first, did you? And then he brought you over here to meet the family, did he? Well, the old man'll be pleased to see you, I can tell you.

RUTH. Good.

LENNY. What did you say?

RUTH. Good.

Pause.

LENNY. Where'd you go to in Italy?

RUTH. Venice.

LENNY. Not dear old Venice? Eh? That's funny. You know, I've always had a feeling that if I'd been a soldier in the last war – say in the Italian campaign – I'd probably have found myself in Venice. I've always had that feeling. The trouble was I was too young to serve, you see. I was only a child, I was too small, otherwise I've got a pretty shrewd idea I'd probably have gone through Venice. Yes, I'd almost certainly have gone through it with my battalion. Do you mind if I hold your hand?

RUTH. Why?

LENNY. Just a touch.

He stands and goes to her.

Just a tickle.

RUTH. Why?

He looks down at her.

LENNY. I'll tell you why.

Slight pause.

One night, not too long ago, one night down by the docks, I was standing alone under an arch, watching all the men jibbing the boom, out in the harbour, and playing about with a yardarm, when a certain lady came up to me and made me a certain proposal. This lady had been searching for me for days. She'd lost tracks of my whereabouts. However, the fact was she eventually caught up with me, and when she caught up with me she made me this certain proposal. Well, this proposal wasn't entirely out of order and normally I would have subscribed to it. I mean I would have subscribed to it in the normal course of events. The only trouble was she was falling apart with the pox. So I turned it down. Well, this lady was very insistent and started taking liberties with me down under this arch, liberties which by any criterion I couldn't be expected to tolerate, the facts being what they were, so I clumped her one. It was on my mind at the time to do away with her, you know, to kill her, and the fact is, that as killings go, it would have been a simple matter, nothing to it. Her chauffeur, who had located me for her, he'd popped round the corner to have a drink, which just left this lady and myself, you see, alone, standing underneath this arch, watching all the steamers steaming up, no one about, all quiet on the Western Front, and there she was up against this wall – well, just sliding down the wall, following the blow I'd given her. Well, to sum up, everything was in my favour, for a killing. Don't worry about the chauffeur. The chauffeur would never have spoken. He was an old friend of the family. But . . . in the end I thought . . . Aaah, why go to all the bother . . . you know, getting rid of the corpse and all that, getting yourself into a state of tension. So I just gave her another belt in the nose and a couple of turns of the boot and sort of left it at that.

RUTH. How did you know she was diseased?

LENNY. How did I know?

Pause.

I decided she was.

Silence.

You and my brother are newly-weds, are you?

RUTH. We've been married six years.

LENNY. He's always been my favourite brother, old Teddy. Do you know that? And my goodness we are proud of him here, I can tell you. Doctor of Philosophy and all that . . . leaves quite an impression. Of course, he's a very sensitive man, isn't he? Ted. Very. I've often wished I was as sensitive as he is.

RUTH. Have you?

LENNY. Oh yes. Oh yes, very much so. I mean, I'm not saying I'm not sensitive. I am. I could just be a bit more so, that's all.

RUTH. Could you?

LENNY. Yes, just a bit more so, that's all.

Pause.

I mean, I am very sensitive to atmosphere, but I tend to get desensitized, if you know what I mean, when people make unreasonable demands on me. For instance, last Christmas I decided to do a bit of snow-clearing for the Borough Council, because we had a heavy snow over here that year in Europe. I didn't have to do this snow-clearing – I mean I wasn't financially embarrassed in any way – it just appealed to me, it appealed to something inside me. What I antici- pated with a good deal of pleasure was the brisk cold bite in the air in the early morning. And I was right. I had to get my snowboots on and I had to stand on a corner, at about five-thirty in the morning, to wait for the lorry to pick me up, to take me to the allotted area. Bloody freezing. Well, the lorry came, I jumped on the tailboard, headlights on, dipped, and off we went. Got there, shovels up, fags on, and off we went, deep into the December snow, hours before cockcrow. Well, that morning, while I was having my mid- morning cup of tea in a neighbouring cafe, the shovel standing by my chair, an old lady approached me and asked me if I would give her a hand with her iron mangle. Her brother-in-law, she said, had left it for her, but he'd left it in the wrong room, he'd left it in the front room. Well, naturally, she wanted it in the back room. It was a present he'd given her, you see, a mangle, to iron out the washing. But he'd left it in the wrong room, he'd left it in the front room, well that was a silly place to leave it, it couldn't stay there. So I took time off to give her a hand. She only lived up the road. Well, the only trouble was when I got there I

couldn't move this mangle. It must have weighed about
half a ton. How this brother-in-law got it up there in the
first place I can't even begin to envisage. So there I was,
doing a bit of shoulders on with the mangle, risking a rupture,
and this old lady just standing there, waving me on, not even
lifting a little finger to give me a helping hand. So after a few
minutes I said to her, now look here, why don't you stuff
this iron mangle up your arse? Anyway, I said, they're out
of date, you want to get a spin drier. I had a good mind to
give her a workover there and then, but as I was feeling
jubilant with the snow-clearing I just gave her a short-arm
jab to the belly and jumped on a bus outside. Excuse me,
shall I take this ashtray out of your way?

RUTH. It's not in my way.

LENNY. It seems to be in the way of your glass. The glass was
about to fall. Or the ashtray. I'm rather worried about the
carpet. It's not me, it's my father. He's obsessed with order
and clarity. He doesn't like mess. So, as I don't believe
you're smoking at the moment, I'm sure you won't object
if I move the ashtray.

He does so.

And now perhaps I'll relieve you of your glass.

RUTH. I haven't quite finished.

LENNY. You've consumed quite enough, in my opinion.

RUTH. No, I haven't.

LENNY. Quite sufficient, in my own opinion.

RUTH. Not in mine, Leonard.

Pause.

LENNY. Don't call me that, please.

RUTH. Why not?

LENNY. That's the name my mother gave me.

Pause.

Just give me the glass.

RUTH. No.

Pause.

LENNY. I'll take it, then.

RUTH. If you take the glass . . . I'll take you.

Pause.

LENNY. How about me taking the glass without you taking me?

RUTH. Why don't I just take you?

Pause.

LENNY. You're joking.

Pause.

You're in love, anyway, with another man. You've had a secret liaison with another man. His family didn't even know. Then you come here without a word of warning and start to make trouble.

She picks up the glass and lifts it towards him.

RUTH. Have a sip. Go on. Have a sip from my glass.

He is still.

Sit on my lap. Take a long cool sip.

She pats her lap. Pause.
She stands, moves to him with the glass.

Put your head back and open your mouth.

LENNY. Take that glass away from me.

RUTH. Lie on the floor. Go on. I'll pour it down your throat.

LENNY. What are you doing, making me some kind of proposal?

She laughs shortly, drains the glass.

RUTH. Oh, I was thirsty.

> *She smiles at him, puts the glass down, goes into the hall and up the stairs.*
> *He follows into the hall and shouts up the stairs.*

LENNY. What was that supposed to be? Some kind of pro-posal?

> *Silence.*
> *He comes back into the room, goes to his own glass, drains it.*
> *A door slams upstairs.*
> *The landing light goes on.*
> MAX *comes down the stairs, in pyjamas and cap. He comes into the room.*

MAX. What's going on here? You drunk?

> *He stares at* LENNY.

What are you shouting about? You gone mad?

> LENNY *pours another glass of water.*

Prancing about in the middle of the night shouting your head off. What are you, a raving lunatic?

LENNY. I was thinking aloud.

MAX. Is Joey down here? You been shouting at Joey?

LENNY. Didn't you hear what I said, Dad? I said I was thinking aloud.

MAX. You were thinking so loud you got me out of bed.

LENNY. Look, why don't you just ... pop off, eh?

MAX. Pop off? He wakes me up in the middle of the night, I think we got burglars here, I think he's got a knife stuck in him, I come down here, he tells me to pop off.

> LENNY *sits down.*

He was talking to someone. Who could he have been talking to? They're all asleep. He was having a conversation with someone. He won't tell me who it was. He pretends he was thinking aloud. What are you doing, hiding someone here?

LENNY. I was sleepwalking. Get out of it, leave me alone, will you?

MAX. I want an explanation, you understand? I asked you who you got hiding here.

Pause.

LENNY. I'll tell you what, Dad, since you're in the mood for a bit of a . . . chat, I'll ask you a question. It's a question I've been meaning to ask you for some time. That night . . . you know . . . the night you got me . . . that night with Mum, what was it like? Eh? When I was just a glint in your eye. What was it like? What was the background to it? I mean, I want to know the real facts about my background. I mean, for instance, is it a fact that you had me in mind all the time, or is it a fact that I was the last thing you had in mind?

Pause.

I'm only asking this in a spirit of inquiry, you understand that, don't you? I'm curious. And there's lots of people of my age share that curiosity, you know that, Dad? They often ruminate, sometimes singly, sometimes in groups, about the true facts of that particular night – the night they were made in the image of those two people *at it*. It's a question long overdue, from my point of view, but as we happen to be passing the time of day here tonight I thought I'd pop it to you.

Pause.

MAX. You'll drown in your own blood.

LENNY. If you prefer to answer the question in writing I've got no objection.

MAX *stands.*

I should have asked my dear mother. Why didn't I ask my dear mother? Now it's too late. She's passed over to the other side.

> MAX *spits at him.*
> LENNY *looks down at the carpet.*

Now look what you've done. I'll have to Hoover that in the morning, you know.

> MAX *turns and walks up the stairs.*
> LENNY *sits still.*
> BLACKOUT.
> LIGHTS UP.

> *Morning.*
> JOEY *in front of the mirror. He is doing some slow limbering-up exercises. He stops, combs his hair, carefully. He then shadowboxes, heavily, watching himself in the mirror.*
> MAX *comes in from* U.L.
> *Both* MAX *and* JOEY *are dressed.* MAX *watches* JOEY *in silence.* JOEY *stops shadowboxing, picks up a newspaper and sits.*
> *Silence.*

MAX. I hate this room.

> *Pause.*

It's the kitchen I like. It's nice in there. It's cosy.

> *Pause.*

But I can't stay in there. You know why? Because he's always washing up in there, scraping the plates, driving me out of the kitchen, that's why.

JOEY. Why don't you bring your tea in here?

MAX. I don't want to bring my tea in here. I hate it here. I want to drink my tea in there.

He goes into the hall and looks towards the kitchen.

What's he doing in there?

He returns.

What's the time?
JOEY. Half past six.
MAX. Half past six.

Pause.

I'm going to see a game of football this afternoon. You want to come?

Pause.

I'm talking to you.
JOEY. I'm training this afternoon. I'm doing six rounds with Blackie.
MAX. That's not till five o'clock. You've got time to see a game of football before five o'clock. It's the first game of the season.
JOEY. No, I'm not going.
MAX. Why not?

Pause.
MAX *goes into the hall.*

Sam! Come here!

MAX *comes back into the room.*
SAM *enters with a cloth.*

SAM. What?
MAX. What are you doing in there?
SAM. Washing up.
MAX. What else?
SAM. Getting rid of your leavings.
MAX. Putting them in the bin, eh?

SAM. Right in.

MAX. What point you trying to prove?

SAM. No point.

MAX. Oh yes, you are. You resent making my breakfast, that's what it is, isn't it? That's why you bang round the kitchen like that, scraping the frying-pan, scraping all the leavings into the bin, scraping all the plates, scraping all the tea out of the teapot . . . that's why you do that, every single stinking morning. I know. Listen, Sam. I want to say something to you. From my heart.

He moves closer.

I want you to get rid of these feelings of resentment you've got towards me. I wish I could understand them. Honestly, have I ever given you cause? Never. When Dad died he said to me, Max, look after your brothers. That's exactly what he said to me.

SAM. How could he say that when he was dead?

MAX. What?

SAM. How could he speak if he was dead?

Pause.

MAX. Before he died, Sam. Just before. They were his last words. His last sacred words, Sammy. You think I'm joking? You think when my father spoke – on his death-bed – I wouldn't obey his words to the last letter? You hear that, Joey? He'll stop at nothing. He's even prepared to spit on the memory of our Dad. What kind of a son were you, you wet wick? You spent half your time doing crossword puzzles! We took you into the butcher's shop, you couldn't even sweep the dust off the floor. We took MacGregor into the shop, he could run the place by the end of a week. Well, I'll tell you one thing. I respected my father not only as a man but as a number one butcher! And

to prove it I followed him into the shop. I learned to carve
a carcass at his knee. I commemorated his name in blood.
I gave birth to three grown men! All on my own bat. What
have you done?

Pause.

What have you done? You tit!

SAM. Do you want to finish the washing up? Look, here's the
cloth.

MAX. So try to get rid of these feelings of resentment, Sam.
After all, we are brothers.

SAM. Do you want the cloth? Here you are. Take it.

> TEDDY *and* RUTH *come down the stairs. They walk across
> the hall and stop just inside the room.*
> *The others turn and look at them.* JOEY *stands.*
> TEDDY *and* RUTH *are wearing dressing-gowns.*
> *Silence.*
> TEDDY *smiles.*

TEDDY. Hullo . . . Dad . . . We overslept.

Pause.

What's for breakfast?

> *Silence.*
> TEDDY *chuckles.*

Huh. We overslept.

> MAX *turns to* SAM.

MAX. Did you know he was here?
SAM. No.

> MAX *turns to* JOEY.

MAX. Did you know he was here?

Pause.

I asked you if you knew he was here.
JOEY. No.
MAX. Then who knew?

Pause.

Who knew?

Pause.

I didn't know.
TEDDY. I was going to come down, Dad, I was going to . .
be here, when you came down.

Pause.

How are you?

Pause.

Uh . . . look, I'd . . . like you to meet . . .
MAX. How long you been in this house?
TEDDY. All night.
MAX. All night? I'm a laughing-stock. How did you get in?
TEDDY. I had my key.

MAX *whistles and laughs.*

MAX. Who's this?
TEDDY. I was just going to introduce you.
MAX. Who asked you to bring tarts in here?
TEDDY. Tarts?
MAX. Who asked you to bring dirty tarts into this house?
TEDDY. Listen, don't be silly –
MAX. You been here all night?
TEDDY. Yes, we arrived from Venice –
MAX. We've had a smelly scrubber in my house all night.
We've had a stinking pox-ridden slut in my house all night.

TEDDY. Stop it! What are you talking about?

MAX. I haven't seen the bitch for six years, he comes home without a word, he brings a filthy scrubber off the street, he shacks up in my house!

TEDDY. She's my wife! We're married!

Pause.

MAX. I've never had a whore under this roof before. Ever since your mother died. My word of honour. (*To* JOEY.) Have you ever had a whore here? Has Lenny ever had a whore here? They come back from America, they bring the slopbucket with them. They bring the bedpan with them. (*To* TEDDY.) Take that disease away from me. Get her away from me.

TEDDY. She's my wife.

MAX (*to* JOEY). Chuck them out.

Pause.

A Doctor of Philosophy, Sam, you want to meet a Doctor of Philosophy? (*To* JOEY.) I said chuck them out.

Pause.

What's the matter? You deaf?

JOEY. You're an old man. (*To* TEDDY.) He's an old man.

LENNY *walks into the room, in a dressing-gown.*
He stops.
They all look round.
MAX *turns back, hits* JOEY *in the stomach with all his might.*
JOEY *contorts, staggers across the stage.* MAX, *with the exertion of the blow, begins to collapse. His knees buckle. He clutches his stick.*
SAM *moves forward to help him.*
MAX *hits him across the head with his stick,* SAM *sits, head in hands.*

JOEY, *hands pressed to his stomach, sinks down at the feet of*
RUTH
She looks down at him.
LENNY *and* TEDDY *are still.*
JOEY *slowly stands. He is close to* RUTH. *He turns from*
RUTH, *looks round at* MAX.
SAM *clutches his head.*
MAX *breathes heavily, very slowly gets to his feet.*
JOEY *moves to him.*
They look at each other.
Silence.
MAX *moves past* JOEY, *walks towards* RUTH. *He gestures
with his stick.*

MAX. Miss.

> RUTH *walks towards him.*

RUTH. Yes?

> *He looks at her.*

MAX. You a mother?
RUTH. Yes.
MAX. How many you got?
RUTH. Three.

> *He turns to* TEDDY.

MAX. All yours, Ted?

> *Pause.*

Teddy, why don't we have a nice cuddle and kiss, eh? Like
the old days? What about a nice cuddle and kiss, eh?
TEDDY. Come on, then.

> *Pause.*

MAX. You want to kiss your old father? Want a cuddle with
your old father?

TEDDY. Come on, then.

TEDDY *moves a step towards him.*

Come on.

Pause.

MAX. You still love your old Dad, eh?

They face each other.

TEDDY. Come on, Dad. I'm ready for the cuddle.

MAX *begins to chuckle, gurgling.*
He turns to the family and addresses them.

MAX. He still loves his father!

Curtain

Act Two

Afternoon.

MAX, TEDDY, LENNY *and* SAM *are about the stage, lighting cigars.*

JOEY *comes in from* U.L. *with a coffee tray, followed by* RUTH. *He puts the tray down.* RUTH *hands coffee to all the men. She sits with her cup.* MAX *smiles at her.*

RUTH. That was a very good lunch.

MAX. I'm glad you liked it. (*To the others.*) Did you hear that? (*To* RUTH.) Well, I put my heart and soul into it, I can tell you. (*He sips.*) And this is a lovely cup of coffee.

RUTH. I'm glad.

Pause.

MAX. I've got the feeling you're a first-rate cook.

RUTH. I'm not bad.

MAX. No, I've got the feeling you're a number one cook. Am I right, Teddy?

TEDDY. Yes, she's a very good cook.

Pause.

MAX. Well, it's a long time since the whole family was together, eh? If only your mother was alive. Eh, what do you say, Sam? What would Jessie say if she was alive? Sitting here with her three sons. Three fine grown-up lads. And a lovely daughter-in-law. The only shame is her grand-children aren't here. She'd have petted them and cooed over them, wouldn't she, Sam? She'd have fussed over them and played with them, told them stories, tickled them – I tell you she'd have been hysterical. (*To* RUTH.) Mind you, she taught those boys everything they know. She taught them all the morality they know. I'm telling you. Every single bit of the moral code they live by – was taught to them by their mother. And she had a heart to go with it. What a heart. Eh, Sam? Listen, what's the use of beating round the bush? That woman was the backbone to this family. I mean, I was busy working twenty-four hours a day in the shop, I was going all over the country to find meat, I was making my way in the world, but I left a woman at home with a will of iron, a heart of gold and a mind. Right, Sam?

Pause.

What a mind.

Pause.

Mind you, I was a generous man to her. I never left her short of a few bob. I remember one year I entered into negotiations with a top-class group of butchers with continental connections. I was going into association with them. I remember the night I came home, I kept quiet. First of all I gave Lenny a bath, then Teddy a bath, then Joey a bath. What fun we used to have in the bath, eh, boys? Then I came downstairs and I made Jessie put her feet up on a pouffe – what happened to that pouffe, I haven't seen it for years – she put her feet up on the pouffe and I said to her, Jessie, I think our ship is going to come home, I'm going to treat you to a couple of items, I'm going to buy you a dress in pale corded blue silk, heavily encrusted in pearls, and for casual wear, a pair of pantaloons in lilac flowered taffeta. Then I gave her a drop of cherry brandy. I remember the boys came down, in their pyjamas, all their hair shining, their faces pink, it was before they started shaving, and they knelt down at our feet, Jessie's and mine. I tell you, it was like Christmas.

Pause.

RUTH. What happened to the group of butchers?

MAX. The group? They turned out to be a bunch of criminals like everyone else.

Pause.

This is a lousy cigar.

He stubs it out.

He turns to SAM.

What time you going to work?

SAM. Soon.

MAX. You've got a job on this afternoon, haven't you?

SAM. Yes, I know.

MAX. What do you mean, you know? You'll be late. You'll lose your job. What are you trying to do, humiliate me?

SAM. Don't worry about me.

MAX. It makes the bile come up in my mouth. The bile – you understand? (*To* RUTH.) I worked as a butcher all my life, using the chopper and the slab, the slab, you know what I mean, the chopper and the slab! To keep my family in luxury. Two families! My mother was bedridden, my brothers were all invalids. I had to earn the money for the leading psychiatrists. I had to read books! I had to study the disease, so that I could cope with an emergency at every stage. A crippled family, three bastard sons, a slutbitch of a wife – don't talk to me about the pain of childbirth – I suffered the pain, I've still got the pangs – when I give a little cough my back collapses – and here I've got a lazy idle bugger of a brother won't even get to work on time. The best chauffeur in the world. All his life he's sat in the front seat giving lovely hand signals. You call that work? This man doesn't know his gearbox from his arse!

SAM. You go and ask my customers! I'm the only one they ever ask for.

MAX. What do the other drivers do, sleep all day?

SAM. I can only drive one car. They can't all have me at the same time.

MAX. Anyone could have you at the same time. You'd bend over for half a dollar on Blackfriars Bridge.

SAM. Me!

MAX. For two bob and a toffee apple.

SAM. He's insulting me. He's insulting his brother. I'm driving a man to Hampton Court at four forty-five.

MAX. Do you want to know who could drive? MacGregor! MacGregor was a driver.

SAM. Don't you believe it.

> MAX *points his stick at* SAM.

MAX. He didn't even fight in the war. This man didn't even fight in the bloody war!

SAM. I did!

MAX. Who did you kill?

> *Silence.*
>
> SAM *gets up, goes to* RUTH, *shakes her hand and goes out of the front door.*
>
> MAX *turns to* TEDDY.

Well, how you been keeping, son?

TEDDY. I've been keeping very well, Dad.

MAX. It's nice to have you with us, son.

TEDDY. It's nice to be back, Dad.

> *Pause.*

MAX. You should have told me you were married, Teddy. I'd have sent you a present. Where was the wedding, in America?

TEDDY. No, Here. The day before we left.

MAX. Did you have a big function?

TEDDY. No, there was no one there.

MAX. You're mad. I'd have given you a white wedding. We'd

have had the cream of the cream here. I'd have been only too glad to bear the expense, my word of honour.

Pause.

TEDDY. You were busy at the time. I didn't want to bother you.

MAX. But you're my own flesh and blood. You're my first born. I'd have dropped everything. Sam would have driven you to the reception in the Snipe, Lenny would have been your best man, and then we'd have all seen you off on the boat. I mean, you don't think I disapprove of marriage, do you? Don't be daft. (*To* RUTH.) I've been begging my two youngsters for years to find a nice feminine girl with proper credentials – it makes life worth living. (*To* TEDDY.) Anyway, what's the difference, you did it, you made a wonderful choice, you've got a wonderful family, a marvellous career . . . so why don't we let bygones by bygones?

Pause.

You know what I'm saying? I want you both to know that you have my blessing.

TEDDY. Thank you.

MAX. Don't mention it. How many other houses in the district have got a Doctor of Philosophy sitting down drinking a cup of coffee?

Pause.

RUTH. I'm sure Teddy's very happy . . . to know that you're pleased with me.

Pause.

I think he wondered whether you would be pleased with me.

MAX. But you're a charming woman.

Pause.

RUTH. I was . . .
MAX. What?

Pause.

What she say?

They all look at her.

RUTH. I was . . . different . . . when I met Teddy . . .
first.
TEDDY. No you weren't. You were the same.
RUTH. I wasn't.
MAX. Who cares? Listen, live in the present, what are you
worrying about? I mean, don't forget the earth's about
five thousand million years old, at least. Who can afford to
live in the past?

Pause.

TEDDY. She's a great help to me over there. She's a wonderful
wife and mother. She's a very popular woman. She's got
lots of friends. It's a great life, at the University . . . you
know . . . it's a very good life. We've got a lovely house
. . . we've got all . . . we've got everything we want. It's
a very stimulating environment.

Pause.

My department . . . is highly successful.

Pause.

We've got three boys, you know.
MAX. All boys? Isn't that funny, eh? You've got three, I've
got three. You've got three nephews, Joey. Joey! You're
an uncle, do you hear? You could teach them how to
box.

Pause.

JOEY (*to* RUTH). I'm a boxer. In the evenings, after work.
I'm in demolition in the daytime.

RUTH. Oh?

JOEY. Yes. I hope to be full time, when I get more bouts.

MAX (*to* LENNY). He speaks so easily to his sister-in-law, do
you notice? That's because she's an intelligent and sym-
pathetic woman.

He leans to her.

Eh, tell me, do you think the children are missing their
mother?

She looks at him.

TEDDY. Of course they are. They love her. We'll be seeing
them soon.

Pause.

LENNY (*to* TEDDY). Your cigar's gone out.

TEDDY. Oh, yes.

LENNY. Want a light?

TEDDY. No. No.

Pause.

So has yours.

LENNY. Oh, yes.

Pause.

Eh, Teddy, you haven't told us much about your Doctorship
of Philosophy. What do you teach?

TEDDY. Philosophy.

LENNY. Well, I want to ask you something. Do you detect a
certain logical incoherence in the central affirmations of
Christian theism?

TEDDY. That question doesn't fall within my province.

LENNY. Well, look at it this way . . . you don't mind my asking you some questions, do you?

TEDDY. If they're within my province.

LENNY. Well, look at it this way. How can the unknown merit reverence? In other words, how can you revere that of which you're ignorant? At the same time, it would be ridiculous to propose that what we *know* merits reverence. What we know merits any one of a number of things, but it stands to reason reverence isn't one of them. In other words, apart from the known and the unknown, what else is there?

Pause.

TEDDY. I'm afraid I'm the wrong person to ask.

LENNY. But you're a philosopher. Come on, be frank. What do you make of all this business of being and not-being?

TEDDY. What do you make of it?

LENNY. Well, for instance, take a table. Philosophically speaking. What is it?

TEDDY. A table.

LENNY. Ah. You mean it's nothing else but a table. Well, some people would envy your certainty, wouldn't they, Joey? For instance, I've got a couple of friends of mine, we often sit round the Ritz Bar having a few liqueurs, and they're always saying things like that, you know, things like: Take a table, take it. All right, I say, *take* it, *take* a table, but once you've taken it, what you going to do with it? Once you've got hold of it, where you going to take it?

MAX. You'd probably sell it.

LENNY. You wouldn't get much for it.

JOEY. Chop it up for firewood.

LENNY looks at him and laughs.

RUTH. Don't be too sure though. You've forgotten something. Look at me. I . . . move my leg. That's all it is. But I

wear . . . underwear . . . which moves with me . . . it
. . . captures your attention. Perhaps you misinterpret. The
action is simple. It's a leg . . . moving. My lips move.
Why don't you restrict . . . your observations to that?
Perhaps the fact that they move is more significant . . .
than the words which come through them. You must bear
that . . . possibility . . . in mind.

> *Silence*
> TEDDY *stands.*

I was born quite near here.

> *Pause.*

Then . . . six years ago, I went to America.

> *Pause.*

It's all rock. And sand. It stretches . . . so far . . . every-
where you look. And there's lots of insects there.

> *Pause.*

And there's lots of insects there.

> *Silence.*
> *She is still.*
> MAX *stands.*

MAX. Well, it's time to go to the gym. Time for your workout,
Joey.
LENNY (*standing*). I'll come with you.

> JOEY *sits looking at* RUTH.

MAX. Joe.

> JOEY *stands. The three go out.*
> TEDDY *sits by* RUTH, *holds her hand.*
> *She smiles at him.*
> *Pause.*

TEDDY. I think we'll go back. Mmnn?

Pause.

Shall we go home?

RUTH. Why?

TEDDY. Well, we were only here for a few days, weren't we? We might as well . . . cut it short, I think.

RUTH. Why? Don't you like it here?

TEDDY. Of course I do. But I'd like to go back and see the boys now.

Pause.

RUTH. Don't you like your family?

TEDDY. Which family?

RUTH. Your family here.

TEDDY. Of course I like them. What are you talking about?

Pause.

RUTH. You don't like them as much as you thought you did?

TEDDY. Of course I do. Of course I . . . like them. I don't know what you're talking about.

Pause.

Listen. You know what time of the day it is there now, do you?

RUTH. What?

TEDDY. It's morning. It's about eleven o'clock.

RUTH. Is it?

TEDDY. Yes, they're about six hours behind us . . . I mean . . . behind the time here. The boys'll be at the pool . . . now . . . swimming. Think of it. Morning over there. Sun. We'll go anyway, mmnn? It's so clean there.

RUTH. Clean.

TEDDY. Yes.

RUTH. Is it dirty here?

TEDDY. No, of course not. But it's cleaner there.

Pause.

Look, I just brought you back to meet the family, didn't I? You've met them, we can go. The fall semester will be starting soon.

RUTH. You find it dirty here?

TEDDY. I didn't say I found it dirty here.

Pause.

I didn't say that.

Pause.

Look. I'll go and pack. You rest for a while. Will you? They won't be back for at least an hour. You can sleep. Rest. Please.

She looks at him.

You can help me with my lectures when we get back. I'd love that. I'd be so grateful for it, really. We can bathe till October. You know that. Here, there's nowhere to bathe, except the swimming bath down the road. You know what it's like? It's like a urinal. A filthy urinal!

Pause.

You liked Venice, didn't you? It was lovely, wasn't it? You had a good week. I mean . . . I took you there. I can speak Italian.

RUTH. But if I'd been a nurse in the Italian campaign I would have been there before.

Pause.

TEDDY. You just rest. I'll go and pack.

TEDDY goes out and up the stairs.

She closes her eyes.
LENNY appears from U.L.
He walks into the room and sits near her.
She opens her eyes.
Silence.

LENNY. Well, the evenings are drawing in.
RUTH. Yes, it's getting dark.

Pause.

LENNY. Winter'll soon be upon us. Time to renew one's wardrobe.

Pause.

RUTH. That's a good thing to do.
LENNY. What?

Pause.

RUTH. I always . . .

Pause.

Do you like clothes?
LENNY. Oh, yes. Very fond of clothes.

Pause.

RUTH. I'm fond . . .

Pause.

What do you think of my shoes?
LENNY. They're very nice.
RUTH. No, I can't get the ones I want over there.
LENNY. Can't get them over there, eh?
RUTH. No . . . you don't get them there.

Pause.

I was a model before I went away.

LENNY. Hats?

Pause.

I bought a girl a hat once. We saw it in a glass case, in a shop. I tell you what it had. It had a bunch of daffodils on it, tied with a black satin bow, and then it was covered with a cloche of black veiling. A cloche. I'm telling you. She was made for it.

RUTH. No . . . I was a model for the body. A photographic model for the body.

LENNY. Indoor work?

RUTH. That was before I had . . . all my children.

Pause.

No, not always indoors.

Pause.

Once or twice we went to a place in the country, by train. Oh, six or seven times. We used to pass a . . . a large white water tower. This place . . . this house . . . was very big . . . the trees . . . there was a lake, you see . . . we used to change and walk down towards the lake . . . we went down a path . . . on stones . . . there were . . . on this path. Oh, just . . . wait . . . yes . . . when we changed in the house we had a drink. There was a cold buffet.

Pause.

Sometimes we stayed in the house but . . . most often . . . we walked down to the lake . . . and did our modelling there.

Pause.

Just before we went to America I went down there. I walked

from the station to the gate and then I walked up the drive. There were lights on . . . I stood in the drive . . . the house was very light.

>TEDDY *comes down the stairs with the cases. He puts them down, looks at* LENNY.

TEDDY. What have you been saying to her?

>*He goes to* RUTH.

Here's your coat.

>LENNY *goes to the radiogram and puts on a record of slow jazz.*

Ruth. Come on. Put it on.
LENNY (*to* RUTH). What about one dance before you go?
TEDDY. We're going.
LENNY. Just one.
TEDDY. No. We're going.
LENNY. Just one dance, with her brother-in-law, before she goes.

>LENNY *bends to her.*

Madam?

>RUTH *stands. They dance, slowly.*
>TEDDY *stands, with* RUTH'S *coat.*
>MAX *and* JOEY *come in the front door and into the room. They stand.*
>LENNY *kisses* RUTH. *They stand, kissing.*

JOEY. Christ, she's wide open.

>*Pause.*

She's a tart.

>*Pause.*

Old Lenny's got a tart in here.

> JOEY *goes to them. He takes* RUTH'S *arm. He smiles at*
> LENNY. *He sits with* RUTH *on the sofa, embraces and kisses*
> *her.*
> *He looks up at* LENNY.

Just up my street.

> *He leans her back until she lies beneath him. He kisses her.*
> *He looks up at* TEDDY *and* MAX.

It's better than a rubdown, this.

> LENNY *sits on the arm of the sofa. He caresses* RUTH'S *hair*
> *as* JOEY *embraces her.*
> MAX *comes forward, looks at the cases.*

MAX. You going. Teddy? Already?

> *Pause.*

Well, when you coming over again, eh? Look, next time you
come over, don't forget to let us know beforehand whether
you're married or not. I'll always be glad to meet the wife.
Honest. I'm telling you.

> JOEY *lies heavily on* RUTH.
> *They are almost still.*
> LENNY *caresses her hair.*

Listen, you think I don't know why you didn't tell me you
were married? I know why. You were ashamed. You thought
I'd be annoyed because you married a woman beneath you.
You should have known me better. I'm broadminded. I'm
a broadminded man.

> *He peers to see* RUTH'S *face under* JOEY, *turns back to*
> TEDDY.

Mind you, she's a lovely girl. A beautiful woman. And a

mother too. A mother of three. You've made a happy woman out of her. It's something to be proud of. I mean, we're talking about a woman of quality. We're talking about a woman of feeling.

JOEY *and* RUTH *roll off the sofa on to the floor.*
JOEY *clasps her.* LENNY *moves to stand above them. He looks down on them. He touches* RUTH *gently with his foot.*
RUTH *suddenly pushes* JOEY *away.*
She stands up.
JOEY *gets to his feet, stares at her.*

RUTH. I'd like something to eat. (*To* LENNY.) I'd like a drink. Did you get any drink?
LENNY. We've got drink.
RUTH. I'd like one, please.
LENNY. What drink?
RUTH. Whisky.
LENNY. I've got it.

Pause.

RUTH. Well, get it.

LENNY *goes to the sideboard, takes out bottle and glasses.*
JOEY *moves towards her.*

Put the record off.

He looks at her, turns, puts the record off.

I want something to eat.

Pause.

JOEY. I can't cook. (*Pointing to* MAX.) He's the cook.

LENNY *brings her a glass of whisky.*

LENNY. Soda on the side?
RUTH. What's this glass? I can't drink out of this. Haven't you got a tumbler?

LENNY. Yes.

RUTH. Well, put it in a tumbler.

He takes the glass back, pours whisky into a tumbler, brings it to her.

LENNY. On the rocks? Or as it comes?

RUTH. Rocks? What do you know about rocks?

LENNY. We've got rocks. But they're frozen stiff in the fridge.

   RUTH *drinks.*

   LENNY *looks round at the others.*

Drinks all round?

He goes to the sideboard and pours drinks.

JOEY *moves closer to* RUTH.

OEY. What food do you want?

   RUTH *walks round the room.*

RUTH (*to* TEDDY). Has your family read your critical works?

MAX. That's one thing I've never done. I've never read one of his critical works.

TEDDY. You wouldn't understand them.

   LENNY *hands drinks all round.*

JOEY. What sort of food do you want? I'm not the cook, anyway.

LENNY. Soda, Ted? Or as it comes?

TEDDY. You wouldn't understand my works. You wouldn't have the faintest idea of what they were about. You wouldn't appreciate the points of reference. You're way behind. All of you. There's no point in my sending you my works. You'd be lost. It's nothing to do with the question of intelligence. It's a way of being able to look at the world. It's a question of how far you can operate on things and not in things. I mean it's a question of your capacity to ally the two, to relate the two, to balance the two. To see, to be able to *see*! I'm the one who can see. That's why I can write my critical works. Might do you good . . . have a look at them . . . see how certain people can view . . . things . . . how certain people can maintain . . . intellectual equilibrium. Intellectual equilibrium. You're just objects. You just . . . move about. I can observe it. I can see what you do. It's the same as I do. But you're lost in it. You won't get me being . . . I won't be lost in it.

BLACKOUT.
LIGHTS UP.
Evening.
TEDDY *sitting, in his coat, the cases by him.* SAM.
Pause.

SAM. Do you remember MacGregor, Teddy?
TEDDY. Mac?
SAM. Yes.
TEDDY. Of course I do.
SAM. What did you think of him? Did you take to him?
TEDDY. Yes. I liked him. Why?

Pause.

SAM. You know, you were always my favourite, of the lads. Always.

Pause.

When you wrote to me from America I was very touched, you know. I mean you'd written to your father a few times but you'd never written to me. But then, when I got that letter from you . . . well, I was very touched. I never told him. I never told him I'd heard from you.

Pause.

(*Whispering.*) Teddy, shall I tell you something? You were always your mother's favourite. She told me. It's true. You were always the . . . you were always the main object of her love.

Pause.

Why don't you stay for a couple more weeks, eh? We could have a few laughs.

LENNY *comes in the front door and into the room.*

LENNY. Still here, Ted? You'll be late for your first seminar.

He goes to the sideboard, opens it, peers in it, to the right and the left, stands.

Where's my cheese-roll?

Pause.

Someone's taken my cheese-roll. I left it there. (*To* SAM.) You been thieving?

TEDDY. I took your cheese-roll, Lenny.

Silence.
SAM *looks at them, picks up his hat and goes out of the front door.*
Silence.

LENNY. You took my cheese roll?
TEDDY. Yes.
LENNY. I made that roll myself. I cut it and put the butter on. I sliced a piece of cheese and put it in between. I put it on a plate and I put it in the sideboard. I did all that before I went out. Now I come back and you've eaten it.
TEDDY. Well, what are you going to do about it?
LENNY. I'm waiting for you to apologize.
TEDDY. But I took it deliberately, Lenny.

LENNY. You mean you didn't stumble on it by mistake?

TEDDY. No, I saw you put it there. I was hungry, so I ate it.

Pause.

LENNY. Barefaced audacity.

Pause.

What led you to be so . . . vindictive against your own brother? I'm bowled over.

Pause.

Well, Ted, I would say this is something approaching the naked truth, isn't it? It's a real cards on the table stunt. I mean, we're in the land of no holds barred now. Well, how else can you interpret it? To pinch your younger brother's specially made cheese roll when he's out doing a spot of work, that's not equivocal, it's unequivocal.

Pause.

Mind you, I will say you do seem to have grown a bit sulky during the last six years. A bit sulky. A bit inner. A bit less forthcoming. It's funny, because I'd have thought that in the United States of America, I mean with the sun and all that, the open spaces, on the old campus, in your position, lecturing, in the centre of all the intellectual life out there, on the old campus, all the social whirl, all the stimulation of it all, all your kids and all that, to have fun with, down by the pool, the Greyhound buses and all that, tons of iced water, all the comfort of those Bermuda shorts and all that, on the old campus, no time of the day or night you can't get a cup of coffee or a Dutch gin, I'd have thought you'd have grown more forthcoming, not less. Because I want you to know that you set a standard for us, Teddy. Your family looks up to you, boy, and you know what it does? It does its best to follow the example you set. Because you're a great source of pride to us. That's why we were so glad to see you come back, to welcome you back to your birthplace. That's why.

Pause.

No, listen, Ted, there's no question that we live a less rich life here than you do over there. We live a closer life. We're busy, of course. Joey's busy with his boxing, I'm busy with my occupation, Dad still plays a good game of poker, and he does the cooking as well, well up to his old standard, and Uncle Sam's the best chauffeur in the firm. But nevertheless we do make up a unit, Teddy, and you're an integral part of it. When we all sit round the backyard having a quiet gander at the night sky, there's always an empty chair standing in the circle, which is in fact yours. And so when you at length return to us, we do expect a bit of grace, a bit of je ne sais quoi, a bit of generosity of mind, a bit of liberality of spirit, to reassure us. We do expect that. But do we get it? Have we got it? Is that what you've given us?

Pause.

TEDDY. Yes.

JOEY *comes down the stairs and into the room, with a newspaper.*

LENNY (*to* JOEY). How'd you get on?
JOEY. Er . . . not bad.
LENNY. What do you mean?

Pause.

What do you mean?
JOEY. Not bad.
LENNY. I want to know what you *mean* – by not bad.
JOEY. What's it got to do with you?
LENNY. Joey, you tell your brother everything.

Pause.

JOEY. I didn't get all the way.
LENNY. You didn't get all the way?

Pause.

(*With emphasis.*) You didn't get all the way?
But you've had her up there for two hours.
JOEY. Well?
LENNY. You didn't get all the way and you've had her up there
for two hours!
JOEY. What about it?

LENNY *moves closer to him.*

LENNY. What are you telling me?
JOEY. What do you mean?
LENNY. Are you telling me she's a tease?

Pause.

She's a tease!

Pause.

What do you think cf that, Ted? Your wife turns out to be
a tease. He's had her up there for two hours and he didn't
go the whole hog.
JOEY. I didn't say she was a tease.
LENNY. Are you joking? It sounds like a tease to me, don't it
to you, Ted?
TEDDY. Perhaps he hasn't got the right touch.
LENNY. Joey? Not the right touch? Don't be ridiculous. He's
had more dolly than you've had cream cakes. He's irresistible.
He's one of the few and far between. Tell him about the
last bird you had, Joey.

Pause.

JOEY. What bird?

LENNY. The last bird! When we stopped the car . . .

JOEY. Oh, that . . . yes . . . well, we were in Lenny's car one night last week . . .

LENNY. The Alfa.

JOEY. And er . . . bowling down the road . . .

LENNY. Up near the Scrubs.

JOEY. Yes, up over by the Scrubs . . .

LENNY. We were doing a little survey of North Paddington.

JOEY. And er . . . it was pretty late, wasn't it?

LENNY. Yes, it was late. Well?

> *Pause.*

JOEY. And then we . . . well, by the kerb, we saw this parked car . . . with a couple of girls in it.

LENNY. And their escorts.

JOEY. Yes, there were two geezers in it. Anyway . . . we got out . . . and we told the . . . two escorts . . . to go away . . . which they did . . . and then we . . . got the girls out of the car . . .

LENNY. We didn't take them over the Scrubs.

JOEY. Oh, no. Not over the Scrubs. Well, the police would have noticed us there . . . you see. We took them over a bombed site.

LENNY. Rubble. In the rubble.

JOEY. Yes, plenty of rubble.

> *Pause.*

Well . . . you know . . . then we had them.

LENNY. You've missed out the best bit. He's missed out the best bit!

JOEY. What bit?

LENNY (*to* TEDDY). His bird says to him, I don't mind, she says, but I've got to have some protection. I've got to have some contraceptive protection. I haven't got any contraceptive protection, old Joey says to her. In that case I won't

do it, she says. Yes you will, says Joey, never mind about the
contraceptive protection.

LENNY *laughs.*

Even my bird laughed when she heard that. Yes, even she
gave out a bit of a laugh. So you can't say old Joey isn't a
bit of a knockout when he gets going, can you? And here
he is upstairs with your wife for two hours and he hasn't
even been the whole hog. Well, your wife sounds like a bit
of a tease to me, Ted. What do you make of it, Joey? You
satisfied? Don't tell me you're satisfied without going the
whole hog?

Pause.

JOEY. I've been the whole hog plenty of times. Sometimes . . .
you can be happy . . . and not go the whole hog. Now and
again . . . you can be happy . . . without going any hog.

LENNY *stares at him.*
MAX *and* SAM *come in the front door and into the room.*

MAX. Where's the whore? Still in bed? She'll make us all
animals.
LENNY. The girl's a tease.
MAX. What?
LENNY. She's had Joey on a string.
MAX. What do you mean?
TEDDY. He had her up there for two hours and he didn't go the
whole hog.

Pause.

MAX. My Joey? She did that to my boy?

Pause.

To my youngest son? Tch, tch, tch, tch. How you feeling,
son? Are you all right?

JOEY. Sure I'm all right.

MAX (*to* TEDDY). Does she do that to you, too?

TEDDY. No.

LENNY. He gets the gravy.

MAX. You think so?

JOEY. No he don't.

Pause.

SAM. He's her lawful husband. She's his lawful wife.

JOEY. No he don't! He don't get no gravy! I'm telling you.
I'm telling all of you. I'll kill the next man who says he gets
the gravy.

MAX. Joey . . . what are you getting so excited about? (*To*
LENNY.) It's because he's frustrated. You see what happens?

JOEY. Who is?

MAX. Joey. No one's saying you're wrong. In fact everyone's
saying you're right.

Pause.

MAX *turns to the others.*

You know something? Perhaps it's not a bad idea to have
a woman in the house. Perhaps it's a good thing. Who knows?
Maybe we should keep her.

Pause.

Maybe we'll ask her if she wants to stay.

Pause.

TEDDY. I'm afraid not, Dad. She's not well, and we've got to
get home to the children.

MAX. Not well? I told you, I'm used to looking after people
who are not so well. Don't worry about that. Perhaps we'll
keep her here.

Pause.

SAM. Don't be silly.

MAX. What's silly?

SAM. You're talking rubbish.

MAX. Me?

SAM. She's got three children.

MAX. She can have more! Here. If she's so keen.

TEDDY. She doesn't want any more.

MAX. What do you know about what she wants, eh, Ted?

TEDDY (*smiling*). The best thing for her is to come home with me, Dad. Really. We're married, you know.

MAX *walks about the room, clicks his fingers.*

MAX. We'd have to pay her, of course. You realize that? We can't leave her walking about without any pocket money. She'll have to have a little allowance.

JOEY. Of course we'll pay her. She's got to have some money in her pocket.

MAX. That's what I'm saying. You can't expect a woman to walk about without a few bob to spend on a pair of stockings.

Pause.

LENNY. Where's the money going to come from?

MAX. Well, how much is she worth? What we talking about, three figures?

LENNY. I asked you where the money's going to come from. It'll be an extra mouth to feed. It'll be an extra body to clothe. You realize that?

JOEY. I'll buy her clothes.

LENNY. What with?

JOEY. I'll put in a certain amount out of my wages.

MAX. That's it. We'll pass the hat round. We'll make a donation. We're all grown-up people, we've got a sense of responsibility. We'll all put a little in the hat. It's democratic.

LENNY. It'll come to a few quid, Dad.

Pause.

I mean, she's not a woman who likes walking around in second-hand goods. She's up to the latest fashion. You wouldn't want her walking about in clothes which don't show her off at her best, would you?

MAX. Lenny, do you mind if I make a little comment? It's not meant to be critical. But I think you're concentrating too much on the economic considerations. There are other considerations. There are the human considerations. You understand what I mean? There are the human considerations. Don't forget them.

LENNY. I won't.

MAX. Well don't.

Pause.

Listen, we're bound to treat her in something approximating, at least, to the manner in which she's accustomed. After all, she's not someone off the street, she's my daughter-in-law!

JOEY. That's right.

MAX. There you are, you see. Joey'll donate, Sam'll donate.
. . .

SAM *looks at him.*

I'll put a few bob out of my pension, Lenny'll cough up. We're laughing. What about you, Ted? How much you going to put in the kitty?

TEDDY. I'm not putting anything in the kitty.

MAX. What? You won't even help to support your own wife? You lousy stinkpig. Your mother would drop dead if she heard you take that attitude.

LENNY. Eh, Dad.

LENNY *walks forward.*

I've got a better idea.

MAX. What?

LENNY. There's no need for us to go to all this expense. I know these women. Once they get started they ruin your budget. I've got a better idea. Why don't I take her up with me to Greek Street?

   Pause.

MAX. You mean put her on the game?

   Pause.

We'll put her on the game. That's a stroke of genius, that's a marvellous idea. You mean she can earn the money herself – on her back?

LENNY. Yes.

MAX. Wonderful. The only thing is, it'll have to be short hours. We don't want her out of the house all night.

LENNY. I can limit the hours.

MAX. How many?

LENNY. Four hours a night.

MAX (*dubiously*). Is that enough?

LENNY. She'll bring in a good sum for four hours a night.

MAX. Well, you should know. After all, it's true, the last thing we want to do is wear the girl out. She's going to have her obligations this end as well. Where you going to put her in Greek Street?

LENNY. It doesn't have to be right in Greek Street, Dad. I've got a number of flats all around that area.

MAX. You have? Well, what about me? Why don't you give me one?

LENNY. You're sexless.

JOEY. Eh, wait a minute, what's all this?

MAX. I know what Lenny's saying. Lenny's saying she can pay her own way. What do you think, Teddy? That'll solve all our problems.

JOEY. Eh, wait a minute. I don't want to share her.

MAX. What did you say?

JOEY. I don't want to share her with a lot of yobs!

MAX. Yobs! You arrogant git! What arrogance. (*To* LENNY.) Will you be supplying her with yobs?

LENNY. I've got a very distinguished clientele, Joey. They're more distinguished than you'll ever be.

MAX. So you can count yourself lucky we're including you in.

JOEY. I didn't think I was going to have to share her!

MAX. Well, you *are* going to have to share her! Otherwise she goes straight back to America. You understand?

Pause.

It's tricky enough as it is, without you shoving your oar in. But there's something worrying me. Perhaps she's not so up to the mark. Eh? Teddy, you're the best judge. Do you think she'd be up to the mark?

Pause.

I mean what about all this teasing? Is she going to make a habit of it? That'll get us nowhere.

Pause.

TEDDY. It was just love play . . . I suppose . . . that's all I suppose it was.

MAX. Love play? Two bleeding hours? That's a bloody long time for love play!

LENNY. I don't think we've got anything to worry about on that score, Dad.

MAX. How do you know?

LENNY. I'm giving you a professional opinion.

LENNY *goes to* TEDDY.

LENNY. Listen, Teddy, you could help us, actually. If I were to send you some cards, over to America . . . you know, very nice ones, with a name on, and a telephone number, very discreet, well, you could distribute them . . . to various parties, who might be making a trip over here. Of course, you'd get a little percentage out of it.

MAX. I mean, you needn't tell them she's your wife.

LENNY. No, we'd call her something else. Dolores, or something.

MAX. Or Spanish Jacky.

LENNY. No, you've got to be reserved about it, Dad. We could call her something nice . . . like Cynthia . . . or Gillian.

Pause.

JOEY. Gillian.

Pause.

LENNY. No, what I mean, Teddy, you must know lots of professors, heads of departments, men like that. They pop over here for a week at the Savoy, they need somewhere they can go to have a nice quiet poke. And of course you'd be in a position to give them inside information.

MAX. Sure. You can give them proper data. I bet you before two months we'd have a waiting list.

LENNY. You could be our representative in the States.

MAX. Of course. We're talking in international terms! By the time we've finished Pan-American'll give us a discount.

Pause.

TEDDY. She'd get old . . . very quickly.

MAX. No . . . not in this day and age! With the health service? Old! How could she get old? She'll have the time of her life.

RUTH *comes down the stairs, dressed.*
She comes into the room.
She smiles at the gathering, and sits.
Silence.

TEDDY. Ruth . . . the family have invited you to stay, for a little while longer. As a . . . as a kind of guest. If you like the idea I don't mind. We can manage very easily at home . . . until you come back.

RUTH. How very nice of them.

Pause.

MAX. It's an offer from our heart.

RUTH. It's very sweet of you.

MAX. Listen . . . it would be our pleasure.

Pause.

RUTH. I think I'd be too much trouble.

MAX. Trouble? What are you talking about? What trouble? Listen, I'll tell you something. Since poor Jessie died, eh, Sam? we haven't had a woman in the house. Not one. Inside this house. And I'll tell you why. Because their mother's image was so dear any other woman would have . . . tarnished it. But you . . . Ruth . . . you're not only lovely and beautiful, but you're kin. You're kith. You belong here.

Pause.

RUTH. I'm very touched.

MAX. Of course you're touched. I'm touched.

Pause.

TEDDY. But Ruth, I should tell you . . . that you'll have to pull your weight a little, if you stay. Financially. My father isn't very well off.

RUTH (*to* MAX). Oh, I'm sorry.

MAX. No, you'd just have to bring in a little, that's all. A few pennies. Nothing much. It's just that we're waiting for Joey to hit the top as a boxer. When Joey hits the top . . . well . . .

Pause.

TEDDY. Or you can come home with me.
LENNY. We'd get you a flat.

Pause.

RUTH. A flat?
LENNY. Yes.
RUTH. Where?
LENNY. In town.

Pause.

But you'd live here, with us.
MAX. Of course you would. This would be your home. In the bosom of the family.
LENNY. You'd just pop up to the flat a couple of hours a night, that's all.
MAX. Just a couple of hours, that's all. That's all.
LENNY. And you make enough money to keep you going here.

Pause.

RUTH. How many rooms would this flat have?
LENNY. Not many.
RUTH. I would want at least three rooms and a bathroom.
LENNY. You wouldn't need three rooms and a bathroom.
MAX. She'd need a bathroom.
LENNY. But not three rooms.

Pause.

RUTH. Oh, I would. Really.
LENNY. Two would do.
RUTH. No. Two wouldn't be enough.

Pause.

I'd want a dressing-room, a rest-room, and a bedroom.

Pause.

LENNY. All right, we'll get you a flat with three rooms and a bathroom.

RUTH. With what kind of conveniences?

LENNY. All conveniences.

RUTH. A personal maid?

LENNY. Of course.

Pause.

We'd finance you, to begin with, and then, when you were established, you could pay us back, in instalments.

RUTH. Oh, no, I wouldn't agree to that.

LENNY. Oh, why not?

RUTH. You would have to regard your original outlay simply as a capital investment.

Pause.

LENNY. I see. All right.

RUTH. You'd supply my wardrobe, of course?

LENNY. We'd supply everything. Everything you need.

RUTH. I'd need an awful lot. Otherwise I wouldn't be content.

LENNY. You'd have everything.

RUTH. I would naturally want to draw up an inventory of everything I would need, which would require your signatures in the presence of witnesses.

LENNY. Naturally.

RUTH. All aspects of the agreement and conditions of employment would have to be clarified to our mutual satisfaction before we finalized the contract.

LENNY. Of course.

Pause.

RUTH. Well, it might prove a workable arrangement.

LENNY. I think so.

MAX. And you'd have the whole of your daytime free, of course. You could do a bit of cooking here if you wanted to.

LENNY. Make the beds.

MAX. Scrub the place out a bit.

TEDDY. Keep everyone company.

> SAM *comes forward.*

SAM (*in one breath*). MacGregor had Jessie in the back of my
cab as I drove them along.

> *He croaks and collapses.*
> *He lies still.*
> *They look at him.*

MAX. What's he done? Dropped dead?

LENNY. Yes.

MAX. A corpse? A corpse on my floor? Get him out of here!
Clear him out of here!

> JOEY *bends over* SAM.

JOEY. He's not dead.

LENNY. He probably was dead, for about thirty seconds.

MAX. He's not even dead!

> LENNY *looks down at* SAM.

LENNY. Yes, there's still some breath there.

MAX (*pointing at* SAM). You know what that man had?

LENNY. Has.

MAX. Has! A diseased imagination.

> *Pause.*

RUTH. Yes, it sounds a very attractive idea.

MAX. Do you want to shake on it now, or do you want to leave
it till later?

RUTH. Oh, we'll leave it till later.

> TEDDY *stands.*
> *He looks down at* SAM.

TEDDY. I was going to ask him to drive me to London Airport.

He goes to the cases, picks one up.

Well, I'll leave your case, Ruth. I'll just go up the road to
the Underground.

MAX. Listen, if you go the other way, first left, first right, you
remember, you might find a cab passing there.

TEDDY. Yes, I might do that.

MAX. Or you can take the tube to Piccadilly Circus, won't
take you ten minutes, and pick up a cab from there out to
the Airport.

TEDDY. Yes, I'll probably do that.

MAX. Mind you, they'll charge you double fare. They'll charge
you for the return trip. It's over the six-mile limit.

TEDDY. Yes. Well, bye-bye, Dad. Look after yourself.

They shake hands.

MAX. Thanks, son. Listen. I want to tell you something. It's
been wonderful to see you.

Pause.

TEDDY. It's been wonderful to see you.

MAX. Do your boys know about me? Eh? Would they like
to see a photo, do you think, of their grandfather?

TEDDY. I know they would.

MAX *brings out his wallet.*

MAX. I've got one on me. I've got one here. Just a minute.
Here you are. Will they like that one?

TEDDY (*taking it*). They'll be thrilled.

He turns to LENNY.

Good-bye, Lenny.

They shake hands.

LENNY. Ta-ta, Ted. Good to see you. Have a good trip.
TEDDY. Bye-bye, Joey.

>JOEY *does not move.*

JOEY. Ta-ta.

>TEDDY *goes to the front door.*

RUTH. Eddie.

>TEDDY *turns.*
>*Pause.*

Don't become a stranger.

>TEDDY *goes, shuts the front door.*
>*Silence.*
>*The three men stand.*
>RUTH *sits relaxed on her chair.*
>SAM *lies still.*
>JOEY *walks slowly across the room.*
>*He kneels at her chair.*
>*She touches his head, lightly.*
>*He puts his head in her lap.*
>MAX *begins to move above them, backwards and forwards.*
>LENNY *stands still.*
>MAX *turns to* LENNY.

MAX. I'm too old, I suppose. She thinks I'm an old man.

>*Pause.*

I'm not such an old man.

>*Pause.*

(*To* RUTH.) You think I'm too old for you?

>*Pause.*

Listen. You think you're just going to get that big slag all

the time? You think you're just going to have him . . .
you're going to just have him all the time? You're going to
have to work! You'll have to take them on, you understand?

Pause.

Does she realize that?

Pause.

Lenny, do you think she understands . . .

He begins to stammer.

What . . . what . . . what . . . we're getting at? What
. . . we've got in mind? Do you think she's got it clear?

Pause.

I don't think she's got it clear.

Pause.

You understand what I mean? Listen, I've got a funny idea
she'll do the dirty on us, you want to bet? She'll use us,
she'll make use of us, I can tell you! I can smell it! You
want to bet?

Pause.

She won't . . . be adaptable!

*He begins to groan, clutches his stick, falls on to his knees by the
side of her chair. His body sags. The groaning stops. His body
straightens. He looks at her, still kneeling.*

I'm not an old man.

Pause.

Do you hear me?

He raises his face to her.

Kiss me.

She continues to touch JOEY'S *head, lightly.*
LENNY *stands, watching.*

Curtain

Tea Party

TEA PARTY was commissioned by sixteen member countries of the European Broadcasting Union, to be transmitted by all of them under the title, *The Largest Theatre in the World*. It was first presented by B.B.C. Television on 25 March 1965 with the following cast:

DISSON	Leo McKern
WENDY	Vivien Merchant
DIANA	Jennifer Wright
WILLY	Charles Gray
DISLEY	John Le Mesurier
LOIS	Margaret Denyer
FATHER	Frederick Piper
MOTHER	Hilda Barry
TOM	Peter Bartlett
JOHN	Robert Bartlett

Directed by Charles Jarrott

A stage version of TEA PARTY, in double-bill with THE BASEMENT, opened at the Duchess Theatre, London, on 17 September 1970, directed by James Hammerstein and produced by Eddie Kulukundis for Knightsbridge Theatrical Productions Ltd, with the following cast:

DISSON	Donald Pleasence
WENDY	Vivien Merchant
DIANA	Gabrielle Drake
WILLY	Barry Foster
TOM	Robin Angell
JOHN	Kevin Chippendale
DISLEY	Derek Aylward
LOIS	Jill Johnson
FATHER	Arthur Hewlett
MOTHER	Hilda Barry

An electric lift rising to the top floor of an office block. WENDY
stands in it.

Corridor.
The lift comes to rest in a broad carpeted corridor, the interior of
an office suite. It is well appointed, silent. The walls are papered
with Japanese silk. Along the walls in alcoves are set, at various
intervals, a selection of individually designed wash basins, water
closets and bidets, all lit by hooded spotlights.
WENDY *steps out of the lift and walks down the corridor towards*
a door. She knocks. It opens.

Disson's office. Morning.
DISSON *rising from a large desk. He goes round the desk to meet*
WENDY *and shakes her hand.*
DISSON. How do you do, Miss Dodd? Nice of you to come.
  Please sit down.
      DISSON *goes back to his seat behind the desk.* WENDY *sits*
      in a chair at the corner of the desk.
  That's right.
      He refers to papers on the desk.
  Well now, I've had a look at your references. They seem to
  be excellent. You've had quite a bit of experience.
WENDY. Yes, sir.
DISSON. Not in my line, of course. We manufacture sanitary
  ware . . . but I suppose you know that?
WENDY. Yes, of course I do, Mr Disson.
DISSON. You've heard of us, have you?
WENDY. Oh yes.
      WENDY *crosses her left leg over her right.*

DISSON. Well, do you think you'd be interested in . . . in this area of work?

WENDY. Oh, certainly, sir, yes, I think I would.

DISSON. We're the most advanced sanitary engineers in the country. I think I can say that quite confidently.

WENDY. Yes, I believe so.

DISSON. Oh yes. We manufacture more bidets than anyone else in England. (*He laughs.*) It's almost by way of being a mission. Cantilever units, hidden cisterns, footpedals, you know, things like that.

WENDY. Footpedals?

DISSON. Instead of a chain or plug. A footpedal.

WENDY. Oh. How marvellous.

DISSON. They're growing more popular every day and rightly so.

WENDY *crosses her right leg over her left.*

Well now, this . . . post is, in fact, that of my personal assistant. Did you understand that? A very private secretary, in fact. And a good deal of responsibility would undoubtedly devolve upon you. Would you . . . feel yourself capable of discharging it?

WENDY. Once I'd correlated all the fundamental features of the work, sir, I think so, yes.

DISSON. All the fundamental features, yes. Good.

WENDY *crosses her left leg over her right.*

I see you left your last job quite suddenly.

Pause.

May I ask the reason?

WENDY. Well, it's . . . a little embarrassing, sir.

DISSON. Really?

Pause.

Well, I think I should know, don't you? Come on, you can tell me. What was it?

WENDY *straightens her skirt over her knees.*

WENDY. Well, it is rather personal, Mr Disson.

DISSON. Yes, but I think I should know, don't you?
Pause.
WENDY. Well, it's simply that I couldn't persuade my chief . . .
to call a halt to his attentions.
DISSON. *What?* (*He consults the papers on the desk.*) A firm of
this repute? It's unbelievable.
WENDY. I'm afraid it's true, sir.
Pause.
DISSON. What sort of attentions?
WENDY. Oh, I don't . . .
DISSON. What sort?
Pause.
WENDY. He never stopped touching me, Mr Disson, that's all.
DISSON. Touching you?
WENDY. Yes.
DISSON. Where? (*Quickly.*) That must have been very dis-
turbing for you.
WENDY. Well, quite frankly, it is disturbing, to be touched all
the time.
DISSON. Do you mean at every opportunity?
WENDY. Yes, sir.
Slight pause.
DISSON. Did you cry?
WENDY. Cry?
DISSON. Did he make you cry?
WENDY. Oh just a little, occasionally, sir.
DISSON. What a monster.
Slight pause.
Well, I do sympathize.
WENDY. Thank you, sir.
DISSON. One would have thought this . . . tampering, this . . .
interfering . . . with secretaries was something of the past, a
myth, in fact, something that only took place in paperback
books. Tch. Tch.
WENDY *crosses her right leg over her left.*

Anyway, be that as it may, your credentials are excellent
and I would say you possessed an active and inquiring
intelligence and a pleasing demeanour, two attributes I con-
sider necessary for this post. I'd like you to start immediately.

WENDY. Oh, that's wonderful. Thank you so much, Mr Disson.

DISSON. Not at all.

They stand. He walks across the room to another desk.

This'll be your desk.

WENDY. Ah.

DISSON. There are certain personal arrangements I'd like you
to check after lunch. I'm . . . getting married tomorrow.

WENDY. Oh, congratulations.

DISSON. Thanks. Yes, this is quite a good week for me, what
with one thing and another.

The telephone rings on his desk.

He crosses and picks it up.

Hullo, Disley. How are you? . . . What? Oh my goodness,
don't say that.

Disson's house. Sitting-room. Evening.

DIANA. This is my brother Willy.

DISSON. I'm very glad to meet you.

WILLY. And I you. Congratulations.

DISSON. Thank you.

DIANA (*giving him a drink*). Here you are, Robert.

DISSON. Thanks. Cheers.

DIANA. Cheers.

WILLY. To tomorrow.

DISSON. Yes.

They drink.

I'm afraid we've run into a bit of trouble.

DIANA. Why?

DISSON. I've lost my best man.

DIANA. Oh no.

DISSON (*to* WILLY). My oldest friend. Man called Disley. Gastric flu. Can't make it tomorrow.

WILLY. Oh dear.

DISSON. He was going to make a speech at the reception – in my honour. A superb speech. I read it. Now he can't make it.
Pause.

WILLY. Isn't there anyone else you know?

DISSON. Yes, of course. But not like him . . . you see. I mean, he was the natural choice.

DIANA. How infuriating.
Pause.

WILLY. Well, look, I can be your best man, if you like.

DIANA. How can you, Willy? You're giving me away.

WILLY. Oh yes.

DISSON. Oh, the best man's not important; you can always get a best man – all he's got to do is stand there; it's the speech that's important, the speech in honour of the groom. Who's going to make the speech?
Pause.

WILLY. Well, I can make the speech, if you like.

DISSON. But how can you make a speech in honour of the groom when you're making one in honour of the bride?

WILLY. Does that matter?

DIANA. No. Why does it?

DISSON. Yes, but look . . . I mean, thanks very much . . . but the fact is . . . that you don't know me, do you? I mean we've only just met. Disley knows me well, that's the thing, you see. His speech centred around our long-standing friendship. I mean, what he knew of my character . . .

WILLY. Yes, of course, of course. No, look, all I'm saying is that I'm willing to have a crack at it if there's no other solution. Willing to come to the aid of the party, as it were.

DIANA. He *is* a wonderful speaker, Robert.

Wedding reception. Private room. Exclusive restaurant.

DISSON, DIANA, WILLY, DISSON'S PARENTS, DISSON'S
SONS. WILLY *is speaking.*

WILLY. I remember the days my sister and I used to swim
together in the lake at Sunderley. The grace of her crawl,
even then, as a young girl. I can remember those long
summer evenings at Sunderley, my mother and I crossing
the lawn towards the terrace and through the great windows
hearing my sister play Brahms. The delicacy of her touch.
My mother and I would, upon entering the music room,
gaze in silence at Diana's long fingers moving in exquisite
motion on the keys. As for our father, our father knew no
pleasure keener than watching his daughter at her needle-
work. A man whose business was the State's, a man eternally
active, his one great solace from the busy world would be to
sit for hours on end at a time watching his beloved daughter
ply her needle. Diana – my sister – was the dear grace of
our household, the flower, the blossom, and the bloom. One
can only say to the groom: Groom, your fortune is im-
measurable.

   Applause. DIANA *kisses him.*

   DISSON *shakes his hand warmly.*

TOASTMASTER. My lords, reverend gentlemen, ladies and
gentlemen, pray silence for Mr William Pierrepoint Torrance, who will propose the toast in honour of the groom.

   WILLY *turns. Applause.*

WILLY. I have not known Robert for a long time, in fact I have
known him only for a very short time. But in that short time
I have found him to be a man of integrity, honesty and
humility. After a modest beginning, he has built his business
up into one of the proudest and most vigorous in the land.
And this – almost alone. Now he has married a girl who
equals, if not surpasses, his own austere standards of
integrity. He has married my sister, who possesses within
her that rare and uncommon attribute known as inner beauty,

not to mention the loveliness of her exterior. Par excellence
as a woman with a needle, beyond excellence as a woman of
taste, discernment, sensibility and imagination. An excellent
swimmer who, in all probability, has the beating of her
husband in the two hundred metres breast stroke.

Laughter and applause.

WILLY *waits for silence.*

It is to our parents that she owes her candour, her elegance
of mind, her *sensibilité*. Our parents, who, though gone, have
not passed from us, but who are here now on this majestic
day, and offer you their welcome, the bride their love, and
the groom their congratulations.

Applause. DIANA *kisses him.*

DISSON *shakes his hand warmly.*

DISSON. Marvellous.

WILLY. Diana, I want to tell you something.

DIANA. What?

WILLY. You have married a good man. He will make you
happy.

DIANA. I know.

DISSON. Wonderful speeches. Wonderful. Listen. What are
you doing these days?

WILLY. Nothing much.

TOASTMASTER. My lords . . .

DISSON (*whispering*). How would you like to come in with me
for a bit? See how you like it, how you get on. Be my second
in command. Office of your own. Plenty of room for initiative.

TOASTMASTER. My lords, reverend gentlemen, ladies and
gentlemen –

WILLY. Marvellous idea. I'll say yes at once.

DISSON. Good.

DIANA *kisses* DISSON.

DIANA. Darling.

TOASTMASTER. Pray silence for the groom.

DISSON *moves forward.*

Applause. Silence.

DISSON. This is the happiest day of my life.

Sumptuous hotel room. Italy.
The light is on. The camera rests at the foot of the bed. The characters are not seen. Their voices heard only.

DISSON. Are you happy?

DIANA. Yes.

DISSON. Very happy?

DIANA. Yes.

DISSON. Have you ever been happier? With any other man?

DIANA. Never.

Pause.

DISSON. I make you happy, don't I? Happier than you've ever been . . . with any other man.

DIANA. Yes. You do.

Pause.

Yes.

Silence.

Disson's house. Workroom.
DISSON *at his workbench. With sandpaper and file he is putting the finishing touches to a home-made model yacht. He completes the job, dusts the yacht, sets it on a shelf and looks at it with satisfaction.*

Disson's house. Breakfast room. Morning.
DISSON *and* DIANA *at the table.*
DISSON. Your eyes are shining.

Pause.

They're shining.

DIANA. Mmmnnn.

DISSON. They've been shining for months.

DIANA (*smiling*). My eyes? Have they?

DISSON. Every morning.

Pause.

I'm glad you didn't marry that . . . Jerry . . . whatever-hisnamewas . . .

DIANA. Oh, him . . .

DISSON. Why didn't you?

DIANA. He was weak.

Pause.

DISSON. I'm not weak.

DIANA. No.

DISSON. Am I?

He takes her hand.

DIANA. You're strong.

THE TWINS *enter the room.*

THE TWINS *mutter,* 'Morning'.

DIANA *and* DISSON *say* 'Good Morning'.

Silence. THE TWINS *sit.* DIANA *pours tea for them. They butter toast, take marmalade, begin to eat.*

Silence.

Would you like eggs?

TOM. No, thanks.

DIANA. John?

Silence.

DISSON. John!

JOHN. What?

DISSON. Don't say what!

JOHN. What shall I say?

DIANA. Would you like eggs?

Pause.

JOHN. Oh.

Pause.

No, thanks.

The boys giggle and eat. Silence.

JOHN *whispers to* TOM.

DISSON. What are you saying? Speak up.

JOHN. Nothing.

DISSON. Do you think I'm deaf?

TOM. I've never thought about it.

DISSON. I wasn't talking to you. I was talking to John.

JOHN. Me? Sorry, sir.

DISSON. Now don't be silly. You've never called me sir before.
That's rather a daft way to address your father.

JOHN. Uncle Willy called his father sir. He told me.

DISSON. Yes, but you don't call *me* sir! Do you understand?

Willy's office. Morning.

DISSON *leads* WILLY *in.*

DISSON. Here you are, Willy. This'll be your office. How'd
you like it?

WILLY. First rate.

DISSON. These two offices are completely cut off from the rest
of the staff. They're all on the lower floor. Our only contact
is by intercom, unless I need to see someone personally,
which is rare. Equally, I dislike fraternization between the
two offices. We shall meet only by strict arrangement, otherwise we'll never get any work done. That suit you?

WILLY. Perfectly.

DISSON. There was a man in here, but I got rid of him.

DISSON *leads* WILLY *through a communicating door into
his own office.*

Disson's office.

On a side table coffee is set for two.

DISSON *goes to the table and pours.*

DISSON. I <u>think</u> I should explain to you the sort of man I am.

I'm a thorough man. I like things to be done and done well. I don't like dithering. I don't like indulgence. I don't like self-doubt. I don't like fuzziness. I like clarity. Clear intention. Precise execution. Black or white?

WILLY. White, please.

DISSON. But I've no patience with conceit and self-regard. A man's job is to assess his powers coolly and correctly and equally the powers of others. Having done this, he can proceed to establish a balanced and reasonable relationship with his fellows. In my view, living is a matter of active and willing participation. So is work. Sugar?

WILLY. Two, please.

DISSON. Now, dependence isn't a word I would use lightly, but I will use it and I don't regard it as a weakness. To understand the meaning of the term dependence is to understand that one's powers are limited and that to live with others is not only sensible but the only way work can be done and dignity achieved. Nothing is more sterile or lamentable than the man content to live within himself. I've always made it my business to be on the most direct possible terms with the members of my staff and the body of my business associates. And by my example opinions are declared freely, without shame or deception. It seems to me essential that we cultivate the ability to operate lucidly upon our problems and therefore be in a position to solve them. That's why your sister loves me. I don't play about at the periphery of matters. I go right to the centre. I believe life can be conducted efficiently. I never waste my energies in any kind of timorous expectation. Neither do I ask to be loved. I expect to be given only what I've worked for. If you make a plum pudding, what do you do with it? You don't shove it up on a shelf. You stick a knife into it and eat it. Everything has a function. In other words, if we're to work together we must appreciate that interdependence is the key word, that it's your job to understand me and mine to understand you. Agreed?

WILLY. Absolutely.

DISSON. Now, the first thing you need is a secretary. We'll get on to it at once.

WILLY. Can I suggest someone? I know she's very keen and, I'd say, very competent.

DISSON. Who?

WILLY. My sister.

Pause.

DISSON. Your sister? You mean my wife?

WILLY. She told me she'd love to do it.

DISSON. She hasn't told me.

WILLY. She's shy.

DISSON. But she doesn't need to work. Why should she want to work?

WILLY. To be closer to you.

Willy's office.

WILLY *and* DIANA *at their desks, both examining folders intently.*
    Silence.

Disson's office.

DISSON *and* WENDY *at their desks.* WENDY *typing on an electric typewriter.* DISSON *looking out of the window.* DISSON *turns from the window, glances at the door leading to* WILLY'S *office. The intercom buzzes on* WENDY'S *desk. She switches through.*

WENDY. Mr Disson does not want to be disturbed until 3.30.

    DISSON *glances again at* WILLY'S *door.*
    Silence.

Disson's house. Sitting-room. Early evening.

DIANA *and* THE TWINS *are sitting about, reading.*

DIANA. Do you miss your mother?

JOHN. We didn't know her very well. We were very young when she died.

DIANA. Your father has looked after you and brought you up very well.

JOHN. Oh, thank you. He'll be pleased to hear that.

DIANA. I've told him.

JOHN. What did he say?

DIANA. He was pleased I thought so. You mean a great deal to him.

JOHN. Children seem to mean a great deal to their parents, I've noticed. Though I've often wondered what 'a great deal' means.

TOM. I've often wondered what 'mean' means.

DIANA. Aren't you proud of your father's achievements?

JOHN. We are. I should say we are.

> *Pause.*

DIANA. And now that your father has married again . . . has the change in your life affected you very much?

JOHN. What change?

DIANA. Living with me.

JOHN. Ah. Well, I think there definitely is an adjustment to be made. Wouldn't you say that, Tom?

DIANA. Of course there is. But would you say it's an easy adjustment to make, or difficult?

JOHN. Well, it really all depends on how good you are at making adjustments. We're very good at making adjustments, aren't we, Tom?

> *The front door slams.* DIANA *and* THE TWINS *look down at their books.* DISSON *comes in. They all look up, smile.*

DISSON. Hullo.

> *They all smile genially at him.*
> DISSON *looks quickly from one to the other.*

Disson's office. Morning.
Sun shining in the window. DISSON *at his desk.* WENDY *at the*
cabinet. He watches her. She turns.

WENDY. Isn't it a beautiful day, Mr Disson?

DISSON. Close the curtains.

    WENDY *closes the curtains.*

Got your pad?

WENDY. Yes, sir.

DISSON. Sit down.

    WENDY *sits in a chair by the corner of his desk.*

Warwick and Sons. We duly acknowledge receipt of your
letter of the twenty-first inst. There should be no difficulty
in meeting your requirements. What's the matter?

WENDY. Sir?

DISSON. You're wriggling.

WENDY. I'm sorry, sir.

DISSON. Is it the chair?

WENDY. Mmn . . . it might be.

DISSON. Too hard, I expect. A little hard for you.

    Pause.

Is that it?

WENDY. A little.

DISSON. Sit on the desk.

WENDY. The desk?

DISSON. Yes, on the leather.

    Slight pause.

It'll be softer . . . for you.

WENDY. Well, that'll be nice.

    Pause. WENDY *eventually uncrosses her legs and stands. She*
    looks at the desk.

I think it's a little high . . . to get up on.

DISSON. Of course it isn't.

WENDY (*looking at the desk*). Hmmmn-mmmn . . .

DISSON. Go on, get up. You couldn't call that high.

WENDY *places her back to the desk and slowly attempts to raise herself up on to it.*

She stops.

WENDY. I think I'll have to put my feet on the chair, really, to hoist myself up.

DISSON. You can hoist yourself up without using your feet.

WENDY (*dubiously*). Well . . .

DISSON. Look, get up or stay down. Make up your mind. One thing or the other. I want to get on with my letter to Birmingham.

WENDY. I was just wondering if you'd mind if I put my high-heeled shoes on your chair . . . to help me get up.

Pause.

DISSON. I don't mind.

WENDY. But I'm worried in case my heels might chip the wood. They're rather sharp, these heels.

DISSON. Are they?

Pause.

Well, try it, anyway. You won't chip the wood.

WENDY *puts her feet on the chair and hoists herself up on to the desk.*

He watches.

WENDY *settles herself on the desk and picks up her pen and pad. She reads from the pad.*

WENDY. There should be no difficulty in meeting your requirements.

Disson's house. Games room. Day.

DISSON *and* WILLY *are playing ping-pong.* THE TWINS *watch.*

A long rally. DISSON *backhand flips to win the point.*

JOHN. Good shot, Dad.

TOM. Thirteen-eighteen.

WILLY. Your backhand's in form, Robert.

JOHN. Attack his forehand.

WILLY *serves. A rally.* WILLY *attacks* DISSON'S *forehand.*
DISSON *moves over to his right and then flips backhand to*
win the point. THE TWINS *applaud.*

TOM. Thirteen-nineteen.

WILLY. Backhand flip on the forehand, eh?

    WILLY *serves.*

    From DISSON'S *point of view see two balls bounce and leap*
    past both ears.

TWINS. Shot!

TOM. Fourteen-nineteen.

    DISSON *puts down his bat and walks slowly to* WILLY.

DISSON. You served two balls, old chap.

WILLY. Two balls?

DISSON. You sent me two balls.

WILLY. No, no. Only one.

DISSON. Two.

    Pause.

JOHN. One, Dad.

DISSON. What?

TOM. One.

    Pause.

    WILLY *walks to* DISSON'S *end, bends.*

WILLY. Look.

    WILLY *picks up one ball.*

  One ball. Catch!

    He throws the ball. DISSON *gropes, loses sight of the ball.*
    It bounces under the table. He crouches, leans under the table
    for it. Gets it, withdraws, looks up. WILLY *and* THE TWINS
    look down at him.

Disley's surgery.
Room darkened.
A torch shining in DISSON'S *eyes. First the left eye, then the right*
eye. Torch out. Light on.

DISLEY. There's nothing wrong with your eyes, old boy.

DISSON. Nothing?

DISLEY. They're in first-rate condition. Truly.

DISSON. That's funny.

DISLEY. I'd go as far as to say your sight was perfect.

DISSON. Huh.

DISLEY. Check the bottom line.

> DISLEY *switches off the light, puts on the light on the letter board.*

What is it?

DISSON. EXJLNVCGTY.

DISLEY. Perfect.

> *Board light off. Room light on.*

DISSON. Yes, I know . . . I know that . . .

DISLEY. Well, what are you worried about?

DISSON. It's not that . . .

DISLEY. Colour? Do you confuse colours? Look at me. What colour am I?

DISSON. Colourless.

DISLEY (*laughs, stops*). Very funny. What distinguishing marks can you see about me?

DISSON. Two.

DISLEY. What?

DISSON. You have one grey strip in your hair, quite faint.

DISLEY. Good. What's the other?

DISSON. You have a brown stain on your left cheek.

DISLEY. A brown stain? Can you see that? (*He looks in the mirror.*) I didn't know it was so evident.

DISSON. Of course it's evident. It stains your face.

DISLEY. Don't . . . go on about it, old boy. I didn't realize it was so evident. No one's ever noticed it before.

DISSON. Not even your wife?

DISLEY. Yes, she has. Anyway, I'd say your eyes are sharp enough. What colour are those lampshades?

DISSON. They're dark blue drums. Each has a golden rim. The carpet is Indian.

DISLEY. That's not a colour.

DISSON. It's white. Over there, by that cabinet, I can see a deep black burn.

DISLEY. A burn? Where? Do you mean that shadow?

DISSON. That's not a shadow. It's a burn.

DISLEY (*looking*). So it is. How the hell did that happen?

DISSON. Listen . . . I never said I couldn't see. You don't understand. Most of the time . . . my eyesight is excellent. It always has been. But . . . it's become unreliable. It's become . . . erratic. Sometimes, quite suddenly, very occasionally, something happens . . . something . . . goes wrong . . . with my eyes.

Pause.

DISLEY. I can find no evidence that your sight is in any way deficient.

DISSON. You don't understand.

A knock at the door. LOIS *appears.*

LOIS. I'm just going out. Wanted to say hullo to you before I go.

DISSON. Hullo, Lois.

He kisses her cheek.

LOIS. You've been in here for ages. Don't tell me you need glasses?

DISLEY. His eyes are perfect.

LOIS. They look it.

DISSON. What a lovely dress you're wearing.

LOIS. Do you like it? Really?

DISSON. Of course I like it.

LOIS. You must see if the birds are still there.

She lifts the blind.

Yes, they are. They're all at the bird bath.

They all look into the garden.

Look at them. They're so happy. They love my bath. They do, really. They love it. They make me so happy, my birds. And they seem to know, instinctively, that I adore them. They do, really.

Disson's house. Bedroom. Night.
DISSON *alone, in front of a mirror.*
He is tying his tie. He ties it. The front end hangs only half-way down his chest.
He unties it, ties it again. The front end, this time, is even shorter.
He unties it, holds the tie and looks at it.
He then ties the tie again. This time the two ends are of equal length.
He breathes deeply, relaxes, goes out of the room.

Disson's house. Dining room. Night.
DIANA, WILLY, DISSON *at dinner.*
DIANA. I'd say she was a real find.
WILLY. Oh, she's of inestimable value to the firm, wouldn't you say, Robert?
DISSON. Oh yes.
DIANA. I mean for someone who's not . . . actually . . . part of us . . . I mean, an outsider . . . to give such devotion and willingness to the job, as she does . . . well, it's remarkable. We were very lucky to find her.
DISSON. I found her, actually.
WILLY. You found me, too, old boy.
DIANA (*laughing*). And me.
     Pause.
She's of course so completely trustworthy, and so very persuasive, on the telephone. I've heard her . . . when the door's been open . . . once or twice.
WILLY. Oh, splendid girl, all round.
DISSON. She's not so bloody marvellous.
     Pause. They look at him.
She's all right, she's all right. But she's not so bloody marvellous.

DIANA. Well, perhaps not quite as accomplished as I am, no.
Do you think I'm a good private secretary, Willy?

WILLY. First rate.

Pause. They eat and drink.

DISSON. I don't think it's a good idea for you to work.

DIANA. Me? Why not? I love it.

DISSON. I never see you. If you were at home I could take the
occasional afternoon off . . . to see you. As it is I never
see you. In day-time.

DIANA. You mean I'm so near and yet so far?

Pause.

DISSON. Yes.

DIANA. Would you prefer me to be your secretary?

DISSON. No, no, of course not. That wouldn't work at all.

Pause.

WILLY. But we do all meet at lunch-time. We meet in the
evening.

DISSON *looks at him.*

DIANA. But I like working. You wouldn't want me to work
for someone else, would you, somewhere else?

DISSON. I certainly wouldn't. You know what Wendy told me,
don't you?

DIANA. What?

DISSON. She told me her last employer was always touching
her.

WILLY. No?

DISSON. Always. Touching her.

DIANA. Her body, you mean?

DISSON. What else?

Pause.

DIANA. Well, if we're to take it that that's general practice,
I think it's safer to stay in the family, don't you? Mind you,
they might not want to touch me in the way they wanted to
touch her.

Pause.

But, Robert, you must understand that I not only want to be your wife, but also your employee. I'm not embarrassing you, am I, Willy?

WILLY. No, of course you're not.

DIANA. Because by being your employee I can help to further your interests, our interests. That's what I want to do. And so does Willy, don't you?

Disson's office. Morning.

DISSON *alone. He stands in the centre of the room. He looks at the door, walks over to* WENDY'S *desk. He looks down at her deskchair. He touches it. Slowly, he sits in it. He sits still.*

The door opens. WENDY *comes in. He stands.*

DISSON. You're late.

WENDY. You were sitting in my chair, Mr Disson.

DISSON. I said you're late.

WENDY. I'm not at all.

WENDY *walks to her desk.*

DISSON *makes way for her. He moves across the room.*

I'm hurt.

DISSON. Why?

WENDY. I've put on my new dress.

He turns, looks at her.

DISSON. When did you put it on?

WENDY. This morning.

Pause.

DISSON. Where?

WENDY. In my flat.

DISSON. Which room?

WENDY. In the hall, actually. I have a long mirror in the hall.

He stands looking at her.

Do you like it?

DISSON. Yes. Very nice.

Disson's house. Workroom.

DISSON. Hold it firmly. You're not holding it firmly.

> TOM *holds a length of wood on the table.* DISSON *chips at its base.*

Use pressure. Grip it.

JOHN. A clamp would be better.

DISSON. A clamp? I want you boys to learn how to concentrate your physical energies, to do something useful.

JOHN. What's it going to be, Dad?

DISSON. You'll find out.

> DISSON *chips. He straightens.*

Give me the saw.

JOHN. Me?

DISSON. The saw! Give me it! (*To* TOM.) What are you doing?

TOM. I'm holding this piece of wood.

DISSON. Well, stop it. I've finished chipping. Look at the point now.

JOHN. If you put some lead in there you could make a pencil out of it.

DISSON. They think you're very witty at your school, do they?

JOHN. Well, some do and some don't, actually, Dad.

DISSON. You. Take the saw.

TOM. Me?

DISSON. I want you to saw it off . . . from here.

> DISSON *makes a line with his finger on the wood.*

TOM. But I can't saw.

JOHN. What about our homework, Dad? We've got to write an essay about the Middle Ages.

DISSON. Never mind the Middle Ages.

JOHN. Never mind the *Middle Ages*?

TOM. Can't you demonstrate how to do it, Dad? Then we could watch.

DISSON. Oh, give me it.

DISSON *takes the saw and points to a mark on the wood.*
Now . . . from here.

TOM (*pointing*). You said from here.

DISSON. No, no, from here.

JOHN (*pointing to the other end*). I could have sworn you said
from there.
    Pause.

DISSON. Go to your room.
    Pause.
Get out.
    JOHN *goes out.* DISSON *looks at* TOM.
Do you want to learn anything?

TOM. Yes.

DISSON. Where did I say I was going to saw it?
    He stares at the wood. TOM *holds it still.*
Hold it still. Hold it. Don't let it move.
    DISSON *saws. The saw is very near* TOM'S *fingers.* TOM
    looks down tensely. DISSON *saws through.*

TOM. You nearly cut my fingers off.

DISSON. No, I didn't . . . I didn't . . .
    He glares suddenly at TOM.
You didn't hold the wood still!

Disson's office.
The curtains are drawn.

DISSON. Come here. Put your chiffon round my eyes. My
eyes hurt.
    WENDY *ties a chiffon scarf round his eyes.*
I want you to make a call to Newcastle, to Mr Martin.
We're still waiting for delivery of goods on Invoice No.
634729. What is the cause for delay?
    WENDY *picks up the telephone, dials, waits.*

WENDY. Could I have Newcastle 77254, please. Thank you.
    She waits. He touches her body.

Yes, I'm holding.

He touches her. She moves under his touch.

Hullo, Mr Martin, please. Mr Disson's office.

Camera on him. His arm stretching.

Mr Martin? Mr Disson's office. Mr Disson . . . Ah, you know what it's about (*She laughs.*) Yes . . . Yes.

Camera on him. He leans forward, his arm stretching.

Oh, it's been dispatched? Oh good. Mr Disson will be glad.

She moves under his touch.

Oh, I will. Of course I will.

She puts the phone down. He withdraws his hand.

Mr Martin sends his apologies. The order has been dispatched.

The intercom buzzes. She switches through. WILLY'S *voice.*
Yes?

WILLY. Oh, Wendy, is Mr Disson there?

WENDY. Did you want to speak to him, Mr Torrance?

WILLY. No. Just ask him if I might borrow your services for five minutes.

WENDY. Mr Torrance wants to know if he might borrow my services for five minutes.

DISSON. What's happened to his own secretary?

WENDY. Mr Disson would like to know what has happened to your own secretary.

WILLY. She's unwell. Gone home. Just five minutes, that's all.

DISSON gestures towards the door.

WENDY. Be with you in a minute, Mr Torrance.

WILLY. Please thank Mr Disson for me.

The intercom switches off.

WENDY. Mr Torrance would like me to thank you for him.

DISSON. I heard.

WENDY *goes through the inner door into* WILLY'S *office, shuts it.*

Silence.

DISSON *sits still, the chiffon round his eyes. He looks towards the door.*

He hears giggles, hissing, gurgles, squeals.

He goes to the door, squats by the handle, raises the chiffon, tries to look through the keyhole. Can see nothing through the keyhole. He drops the chiffon, puts his ear to the door. The handle presses into his skull. The sounds continue. Sudden silence.

The door has opened.

A pair of woman's legs stand by his squatting body.

He freezes, slowly puts forward a hand, touches a leg. He tears the chiffon from his eyes. It hangs from his neck. He looks up.

DIANA *looks down at him.*

Behind her, in the other room, WENDY *is sitting, taking dictation from* WILLY, *who is standing.*

DIANA. What game is this?

He remains.

Get up. What are you doing? What are you doing with that scarf? Get up from the floor. What are you doing?

DISSON. Looking for something.

DIANA. What?

WILLY *walks to the door, smiles, closes the door.*

What were you looking for? Get up.

DISSON (*standing*). Don't speak to me like that. How dare you speak to me like that? I'll knock your teeth out.

She covers her face.

What were you doing in there? I thought you'd gone home. What were you doing in there?

DIANA. I came back.

DISSON. You mean you were in there with both of them? In there with both of them?

DIANA. Yes! So what?

Pause.

DISSON (*calmly*). I was looking for my pencil, which had rolled off my desk. Here it is. I found it, just before you came in, and put it in my pocket. My eyes hurt. I borrowed Wendy's scarf, to calm my eyes. Why are you getting so excited?

Disson's office. Day.
DISSON *at his desk, writing.* WENDY *walks to the cabinet, examines a file. Silence.*
DISSON. What kind of flat do you have, Wendy?
WENDY. Quite a small one, Mr Disson. Quite pleasant.
DISSON. Not too big for you, then? Too lonely?
WENDY. Oh no, it's quite small. Quite cosy.
DISSON. Bathroom fittings any good?
WENDY. Adequate, Mr Disson. Not up to our standard.
   Pause.
DISSON. Live there alone, do you?
WENDY. No, I share it with a girl friend. But she's away quite a lot of the time. She's an air hostess. She wants me to become one, as a matter of fact.
DISSON. Listen to me, Wendy. Don't ever . . . dream of becoming an air hostess. Never. The glamour may dazzle from afar, but, believe you me, it's a mess of a life . . . a mess of a life . . .
   He watches WENDY *walk to her desk with a file and then back to the cabinet.*
Were you lonely as a child?
WENDY. No.
DISSON. Nor was I. I had quite a lot of friends. True friends. Most of them live abroad now, of course – banana planters, oil engineers, Jamaica, the Persian Gulf . . . but if I were to meet them tomorrow, you know . . . just like that . . . there'd be no strangeness, no awkwardness at all. We'd continue where we left off, quite naturally.
   WENDY *bends low at the cabinet.*
   He stares at her buttocks.

It's a matter of a core of affection, you see . . . a core of undying affection . . .

Suddenly WENDY'S *body appears in enormous close-up. Her buttocks fill the screen.*

His hands go up to keep them at bay.

His elbow knocks a round table lighter from his desk.

Picture normal.

WENDY *turns from the cabinet, stands upright.*

WENDY. What was that?

DISSON. My lighter.

She goes to his desk.

WENDY. Where is it?

She kneels, looks under the desk. The lighter is at his feet. She reaches for it. He kicks it across the room.

(*Laughing.*) Oh, Mr Disson, why did you do that?

She stands. He stands. She goes towards the lighter. He gets to it before her, stands with it at his feet. He looks at her. She stops.

What's this?

DISSON *feints his body, left to right*

DISSON. Come on.

WENDY. What?

DISSON. Tackle me. Get the ball.

WENDY. What do I tackle with?

DISSON. Your feet.

She moves forward deliberately.

He dribbles away, turns, kicks the lighter along the carpet towards her. Her foot stops the lighter. She turns with it at her foot.

Ah!

She stands, legs apart, the lighter between them, staring at him.

She taps her foot.

WENDY. Come on, then!

He goes towards her. She eludes him. He grasps her arm.

That's a foul!

He drops her arm.

DISSON. Sorry.

She stands with the lighter between her feet.

WENDY. Come on, come on. Tackle me, tackle me. Come on, tackle me! Get the ball! Fight for the ball!

He begins to move, stops, sinks to the floor. She goes to him. What's the matter?

DISSON. Nothing. All right. Nothing.

WENDY. Let me help you up.

DISSON. No. Stay. You're very valuable in this office. Good worker. Excellent. If you have any complaints, just tell me. I'll soon put them right. You're a very efficient secretary. Something I've always needed. Have you everything you want? Are your working conditions satisfactory?

WENDY. Perfectly.

DISSON. Oh good. Good . . . Good.

Disson's house. Bedroom. Night

DISSON *and* DIANA *in bed, reading. She looks at him.*

DIANA. You seem a little subdued . . . lately.

DISSON. Me? Not at all. I'm reading the Life of Napoleon, that's all.

DIANA. No, I don't mean now, I mean generally. Is there – ?

DISSON. I'm not at all subdued. Really.

Pause.

DIANA. It's our first anniversary next Wednesday, did you know that?

DISSON. Of course I did. How could I forget? We'll go out together in the evening. Just you and I. Alone.

DIANA. Oh. Good.

DISSON. I'm also giving a little tea party in the office, in the afternoon. My mother and father'll be up.

DIANA. Oh good.

Pause.

DISSON. How have you enjoyed our first year?

DIANA. It's been wonderful. It's been a very exciting year.

Pause.

DISSON. You've been marvellous with the boys.

DIANA. They like me.

DISSON. Yes, they do. They do.

Pause.

It's been a great boon, to have you work for the firm.

DIANA. Oh, I'm glad. I am glad.

Pause.

Be nice to get away to Spain.

Pause.

DISSON. You've got enough money, haven't you? I mean, you have sufficient money to see you through, for all you want?

DIANA. Oh yes. I have, thank you.

Pause.

DISSON. I'm very proud of you, you know.

DIANA. I'm proud of you.

Silence.

Disson's office.

DISSON. Have you written to Corley?

WENDY. Yes, Mr Disson.

DISSON. And Turnbull?

WENDY. Yes, Mr Disson.

DISSON. And Erverley?

WENDY. Yes, Mr Disson.

DISSON. Carbon of the Erverley letter, please.

WENDY. Here you are, Mr Disson.

DISSON. Ah. I see you've spelt Erverley right.

WENDY. Right?

DISSON. People tend, very easily, to leave out the first R and call him Everley. You haven't done that.

WENDY. No. (*She turns.*)

DISSON. Just a minute. How did you spell Turnbull? You needn't show me. Tell me.

WENDY. TURNBULL.

DISSON. Quite correct.

Pause.

Quite correct. Now what about – ?

The screen goes black.

Where are you?

Pause.

I can't see you.

WENDY. I'm here, Mr Disson.

DISSON. Where?

WENDY. You're looking at me, Mr Disson.

DISSON. You mean my eyes are open?

Pause.

WENDY. I'm where I was. I haven't moved.

DISSON. Are my eyes open?

WENDY. Mr Disson, really . . .

DISSON. Is this you? This I feel?

WENDY. Yes.

DISSON. What, all this I can feel?

WENDY. You're playing one of your games, Mr Disson. You're being naughty again.

Vision back.

DISSON *looks at her.*

You sly old thing.

Disley's surgery.

A torch shines in DISSON'S *eyes, first right, then left. Torch out.*

Light on.

DISLEY. There's nothing wrong with them.

DISSON. What then?

DISLEY. I only deal with eyes, old chap. Why do you come to me? Why don't you go to someone else?

DISSON. Because it's my eyes that are affected.

DISLEY. Look. Why don't you go to someone else?

> DISLEY *begins to clear away his instruments.*

Nothing worrying you, is there?

DISSON. Of course not. I've got everything I want.

DISLEY. Getting a holiday soon?

DISSON. Going to Spain.

DISLEY. Lucky man.

> *Pause.*

DISSON. Look. Listen. You're my oldest friend. You were going to be the best man at my wedding.

DISLEY. That's right.

DISSON. You wrote a wonderful speech in my honour.

DISLEY. Yes.

DISSON. But you were ill. You had to opt out.

DISLEY. That's right.

> *Pause.*

DISSON. Help me.

> *Pause.*

DISLEY. Who made the speech? Your brother-in-law, wasn't it?

DISSON. I don't want you to think I'm not a happy man. I am.

DISLEY. What sort of speech did he make?

Disson's house. Sitting-room. Evening.

DISSON. Tell me about Sunderley.

WILLY. Sunderley?

DISSON. Tell me about the place where you two were born. Where you played at being brother and sister.

WILLY. We didn't have to play at being brother and sister. We were brother and sister.

DIANA. Stop drinking.

DISSON. Drinking? You call this drinking? This? I used to down eleven or nine pints a night! Eleven or nine pints! Every night of the stinking week! Me and the boys! The boys! And me! I'd break any man's hand for . . . for playing me false. That was before I became a skilled craftsman. That was before . . .

He falls silent, sits.

WILLY. Sunderley was beautiful.

DISSON. I know.

WILLY. And now it's gone, for ever.

DISSON. I never got there.

DISSON stands, goes to get a drink.

He turns from drinks table.

What are you whispering about? Do you think I don't hear? Think I don't see? I've got my memories, too. Long before this.

WILLY. Yes, Sunderley was beautiful.

DISSON. The lake.

WILLY. The lake.

DISSON. The long windows.

WILLY. From the withdrawing-room.

DISSON. On to the terrace.

WILLY. Music playing.

DISSON. On the piano.

WILLY. The summer nights. The wild swans.

DISSON. What swans? What bloody swans?

WILLY. The owls.

DISSON. Negroes at the gate, under the trees.

WILLY. No Negroes.

DISSON. Why not?

WILLY. We had no Negroes.

DISSON. Why in God's name not?

WILLY. Just one of those family quirks, Robert.

DIANA (*standing*). Robert.

Pause.

Come to bed.

DISSON. You can say that, in front of him?

DIANA. Please.

DISSON. In front of *him*?

He goes to her.

Why did you marry me?

DIANA. I admired you. You were so positive.

DISSON. You loved me.

DIANA. You were kind.

DISSON. You loved me for that?

DIANA. I found you admirable in your clarity of mind, your surety of purpose, your will, the strength your achievements had given you –

DISSON. And you adored me for it?

WILLY (*to* DISSON). Can I have a private word with you?

DISSON. You *adored* me for it?

Pause.

DIANA. You know I did.

WILLY. Can I have a private word with you, old chap? (*To* DIANA.) Please.

DIANA *goes out of the room.*

DISSON *looks at* WILLY.

DISSON. Mind how you tread, Bill. Mind . . . how you tread, old Bill, old boy, old Bill.

WILLY. Listen. I've been wondering. Is there anything on your mind?

DISSON. My mind? No, of course not.

WILLY. You're not dissatisfied with my work, or anything?

DISSON. Quite the contrary. Absolutely the contrary.

WILLY. Oh good. I like the work very much. Try to do my best.

DISSON. Listen. I want you to be my partner. Hear me? I want you to share full responsibility . . . with me.

WILLY. Do you really?

DISSON. Certainly.

WILLY. Well, thank you very much. I don't know what to say.

DISSON. Don't say anything.

Disson's office.

WILLY *at the door.*

WILLY. Coming, old chap?

DISSON. Yes.

WILLY (*to* WENDY). Important lunch, this. But I think we'll swing it, don't you, Robert? (*To* WENDY.) Great prospects in store.

> DISSON *and* WILLY *go out.* WENDY *clips some papers together.*

> DIANA *comes in through the inner door.*

WENDY. Oh, hullo, Mrs Disson.

DIANA. Hullo, Wendy.

> *Pause.*

> DIANA *watches* WENDY *clip the papers.*

Do you like being a secretary?

WENDY. I do, yes. Do you?

DIANA. I do, yes.

> *Pause.*

I understand your last employer touched your body . . . rather too much.

WENDY. It wasn't a question of too much, Mrs Disson. One touch was enough for me.

DIANA. Oh, you left after the first touch?

WENDY. Well, not quite the first, no.

> *Pause.*

DIANA. Have you ever asked yourself why men will persist in touching women?

WENDY. No, I've never asked myself that, Mrs Disson.

DIANA. Few women do ask themselves that question.

WENDY. Don't they? I don't know. I've never spoken to any other women on the subject.

DIANA. You're speaking to me.

WENDY. Yes. Well, have you ever asked yourself that question, Mrs Disson?

DIANA. Never. No.

Pause.

Have lunch with me today. Tell me about yourself.

WENDY. I'll have lunch with you with pleasure.

DISSON comes in. They look at him. He at them. Silence.

DISSON. Forgotten . . . one of the designs.

DIANA smiles at him. WENDY clips her papers. He goes to his desk, collects a folder, stands upright.

DIANA looks out of the window. WENDY clips papers. He looks at them, goes out. DIANA and WENDY remain silent.

Disson's house. Games room.

DISSON and WILLY playing ping-pong. They are in the middle of a long rally. THE TWINS watch. WILLY is on the attack, DISSON playing desperately, retrieving from positions of great difficulty. He cuts, chops, pushes.

TWINS (*variously*). Well done, Dad. Good shot, Dad. Good one, Dad.

WILLY forces DISSON on to the forehand. He slams viciously. DISSON skids.

The screen goes black.

Good shot!

DISSON. Aaah!

Vision back.

DISSON is clutching the table, bent over it.

WILLY *throws the ball on to the table.*

It bounces gently across it.

Disson's house. Sitting-room. Evening.

DISSON'S *parents.*

MOTHER. Have I seen that mirror before?

DISSON. No. It's new.

MOTHER. I knew I hadn't seen it. Look at it, John. What a beautiful mirror.

FATHER. Must have cost you a few bob.

MOTHER. Can you see the work on it, John? I bet it must be a few years old, that mirror.

DISSON. It's a few hundred years old.

FATHER. I bet it must have cost you a few bob.

DISSON. It wasn't cheap.

FATHER. Cheap?

MOTHER. What a beautiful mirror.

FATHER. Cheap? Did you hear what he said, Dora? He said it wasn't cheap!

MOTHER. No, I bet it wasn't.

FATHER (*laughing*). Cheap!

   Pause.

MOTHER. Mrs Tidy sends you her love.

DISSON. Who?

FATHER. Mrs Tidy. The Tidys.

DISSON. Oh yes. How are they?

FATHER. Still very tidy. (*Laughs.*) Aren't they, Dora?

MOTHER. You remember the Tidys.

DISSON. Of course I remember them.

   Pause.

How have you been keeping, then?

FATHER. Oh, your mother's had a few pains. You know, just a few.

MOTHER. Only a few, John. I haven't had many pains.

FATHER. I only said you'd had a few. Not many.

   Pause.

MOTHER. Are the boys looking forward to their holiday?

DISSON. Yes, they are.

FATHER. When are you going?

DISSON. I'm not.

head.
f door opening and closing, muffled steps, an odd cough,
of teacups, whispers.

proaches.

head.
f door opening and closing, muffled steps, an odd cough,
of teacups, whispers.

ble has been set out. Two ELDERLY LADIES *serve*
ches, bridge rolls, buns and cakes. The gathering is
und the table in silence. DISLEY *whispers to them.*
is eyes are a little strained, that's all. Just resting
n't mention it. It'll embarrass him. It's quite all

ll take their tea, choose edibles, and relax.
sing a cake). These are good.
are they?
osing a bridge roll). These look nice.
ook wonderful, Mrs Disson. Absolutely wonderful.
he, Peter?
arvellous.
do you think of your grandsons?
hey've grown up now, haven't they?

Disson's office.
DISSON. Tighter.
   WENDY *ties the chiffon round his eyes.*
WENDY. There. You look nice.
DISSON. This chiffon stinks.
WENDY. Oh, I do apologize. What of?
   Pause.
You're very rude to me. But you do look nice. You really do.
   DISSON *tears the chiffon off.*
DISSON. It's useless. Ring Disley. Tell him to come here.
WENDY. But he'll be here at four o'clock, for your tea party.
DISSON. I want him now! I want him . . . now.
WENDY. Don't you like my chiffon any more, to put round your eyes? My lovely chiffon?
   Pause.
   He sits still.
I always feel like kissing you when you've got that on round your eyes. Do you know that? Because you're all in the dark.
   Pause.
Put it on.
   She picks up the chiffon and folds it.
I'll put it on . . . for you. Very gently.
   She leans forward.
   He touches her.
No – you mustn't touch me, if you're not wearing your chiffon.
   She places the chiffon on his eyes.
   He trembles, puts his hand to the chiffon, slowly lowers it, lets it fall.
   It flutters to the floor.
   As she looks at him, he reaches for the telephone.

Disson's office.
DISSON *in the same position.*
DISSON. I need a tight bandage. Very tight.
DISLEY. Anyone could do that for you.
DISSON. No. You're my eye consultant. You must do it for me.
DISLEY. All right.
>He takes a bandage from his case and ties it round DISSON'S eyes.

Just for half an hour. You don't want it on when your guests arrive, do you?
>DISLEY *ties the knots.*

This'll keep you in the dark, all right. Also lend pressure to your temples. Is that what you want?
DISSON. That's it. That's what I want.
>DISLEY *cuts the strands.*

DISLEY. There. How's that?
>*Pause.*
>See anything?

Disson's office. Afternoon.
DISSON *sits alone, the bandage round his eyes.*
Silence.
WILLY *enters from his office. He sees* DISSON *and goes to him.*
WILLY. How are you, old chap? Bandage on straight? Knots tight?
>He pats him on the back and goes out through the front office door.
>*The door slams.*
>DISSON *sits still.*

Corridor.
MR *and* MRS DISLEY *approaching the office.*

LOIS. Why didn't he make it party, of all things?
DISLEY. I couldn't say.

Office.
DISSON'S *head.*
Soft clicks of door opening and closing slight rattle of teacups.

Corridor.
DISSON'S *parents approaching the off*
MOTHER. I could do with a cup of t

Office.
DISSON'S *head.*
Soft clicks of door opening and closing cough, slight rattle of teacups.

Corridor.
THE TWINS *approach, silent.*

Office.
DISSON'S *head.*
Soft clicks of door opening and closing, muffle slight rattle of teacups, a short whisper.

Corridor.
DIANA *and* WILLY *approach.*
DIANA. Why *don't* you come to Spain with
WILLY. I think I will.

LOIS. Of course, we knew them when they were that high, didn't we, Tom?

FATHER. So did we.

TOM. Yes.

WILLY. Big lads now, aren't they, these two?

JOHN. Cake, Granny?

MOTHER. No, I've had one.

JOHN. Have two.

FATHER. I'll have one.

MOTHER. He's had one.

FATHER. I'll have two.

> WENDY *takes a cup of tea to* DISSON *and puts it into his hands.*

WENDY. Here's a cup of tea, Mr Disson. Drink it. It's warm.

LOIS (*to* DIANA). You're off to Spain quite soon, aren't you, Diana?

DIANA. Yes, quite soon.

DISLEY (*calling*). We'll take off those bandages in a minute, old chap!

LOIS. Spain is wonderful at this time of the year.

WILLY. Any time of the year, really.

LOIS. But I think it's best at this time of the year, don't you?

DIANA. What sun lotion do you use, Lois?

DISSON'S *point of view.*
No dialogue is heard in all shots from DISSON'S *point of view. Silence.*
Figures mouthing silently, in conspiratorial postures, seemingly whispering together.

Shot including DISSON.

TOM. I went into goal yesterday.

WILLY. How did you do?

LOIS. You can get it anywhere. It's perfect.

JOHN. He made two terrific saves.

TOM. The first was a fluke.

LOIS. How do you sun, then?

DIANA. I have to be rather careful.

TOM. Second save wasn't a bad save.

LOIS. How do you sun, Wendy?

WENDY. Oh not too bad, really.

LOIS (*to* MRS DISSON). We go to our little island every year
    and when we go we have to leave our poor little Siamese with
    my mother.

MOTHER. Do you really?

LOIS. They're almost human, aren't they, Siamese?

DIANA. I'm sure my Siamese was.

LOIS. Aren't they, Peter, almost human?

DIANA. Wasn't Tiger a human cat, Willy, at Sunderley?

WILLY. He adored you.

DISLEY. They really are almost human, aren't they, Siamese?

DISSON'S *point of view.*
Silence.
The party splits into groups. Each group whispering.
The two ELDERLY LADIES *at the buffet table.*
DISSON'S PARENTS, *sitting together.*
THE TWINS *and the* DISLEYS.
WILLY, WENDY *and* DIANA *in a corner.*

Shot including DISSON.
The gathering in a close group, the PARENTS *sitting.*
LOIS. I'd go like a shot.

WENDY. What, me? Come to Spain?

DIANA. Yes, why not?

     WILLY *leans across* DISLEY.

WILLY. Yes, of course you must come. Of course you must
   come.
WENDY. How wonderful.

DISSON'S *point of view.*
WILLY *approaches* DISSON. *With a smile, he takes a ping-pong
ball from his pocket, and puts it into* DISSON'S *hand.*
DISSON *clutches it.*

DISSON'S *point of view.*
WILLY *returns to* WENDY *and* DIANA, *whispers to them.*
DIANA *laughs (silently), head thrown back, gasps with laughter.*
WENDY *smiles.*
WILLY *puts one arm round* WENDY, *the other round* DIANA.
He leads them to WENDY'S *desk.*
WILLY *places cushions on the desk.*
DIANA *and* WENDY, *giggling silently, hoist themselves up on to
the desk. They lie head to toe.*

DISSON'S *point of view. Close-up.*
WENDY'S *face.* WILLY'S *fingers caressing it.* DIANA'S *shoes in
background.*

DISSON'S *point of view. Close-up.*
DIANA'S *face.* WILLY'S *fingers caressing it.* WENDY'S *shoes in
background.*

DISSON'S *point of view.*
LOIS *powdering her nose.*

DISSON'S *point of view.*
The ELDERLY LADIES *drinking tea, at the table.*

DISSON'S *point of view.*
DISLEY *talking to the boys by the window.* THE TWINS *listening intently.*

DISSON'S *point of view.*
DISSON'S PARENTS *sitting, dozing.*

DISSON'S *point of view.*
The base of WENDY'S *desk.*
A shoe drops to the floor.

Shot including DISSON.
DISSON *falls to the floor in his chair with a crack. His teacup drops and spills.*
The gathering is grouped by the table, turns.
DISLEY *and* WILLY *go to him.*
They try to lift him from the chair, are unable to do so.
DISLEY *cuts the bandage and takes it off.*
DISSON'S *eyes are open.*
DISLEY *feels his pulse.*
DISLEY. He's all right. Get him up.

> DISLEY *and* WILLY *try to pull him up from the chair, are unable to do so.*
>
> JOHN *and* TOM *join them.*

Get it up.

*The four of them, with great effort, manage to set the chair
on its feet.*
DISSON *is still seated.*
He must lie down. Now, two hold the chair, and two pull
him.
> JOHN *and* WILLY *hold the chair.*
> DISLEY *and* TOM *pull.*

The chair.
The chair scrapes, moves no farther.

The group around the chair.
They pull, with great effort.

The chair.
The chair scrapes, moves no farther.

The room.
WILLY. Anyone would think he was chained to it!
DISLEY (*pulling*). Come out!
MOTHER. Bobbie!
> *They stop pulling.*
> DISSON *in the chair, still, his eyes open.*
> DIANA *comes to him.*
> *She kneels by him.*
DIANA. This is . . . Diana.
> *Pause.*
Can you hear me?
> *Pause.*
Can he see me?
> *Pause.*

Robert.
>*Pause.*

Can you hear me?
>*Pause.*

Robert, can you see me?
>*Pause.*

It's me. It's me, darling.
>*Slight pause.*

It's your wife.

DISSON'S *face in close-up.*
DISSON'S *eyes. Open.*

The Basement

THE BASEMENT was first presented by B.B.C. Television on 20 February 1967 with the following cast:

STOTT	Harold Pinter
JANE	Kika Markham
LAW	Derek Godfrey

Directed by Charles Jarrott

A stage version of THE BASEMENT, in double-bill with TEA PARTY, opened at the Duchess Theatre, London, on 17 September 1970, directed by James Hammerstein and produced by Eddie Kulukundis for Knightsbridge Theatrical Productions Ltd, with the following cast:

LAW	Donald Pleasence
STOTT	Barry Foster
JANE	Stephanie Beacham

Exterior. Front area of a basement flat.
Winter. Night.
Rain falling.
Short stone flight of steps from street.
Light shining through the basement door.
The upper part of the house is dark.
The back of a man, STOTT. *He stands in the centre of the area,*
looking towards the door.
He wears a raincoat, his head is bare.

Exterior. Front area.
STOTT'S *face. Behind him, by the wall, a girl,* JANE. *She is*
huddled by the wall. She wears a rainhat, clasps her raincoat to
her.

Interior. Room.
The room is large and long. A window at one end looks out to a
small concrete yard. There are doors to bathroom and kitchen.
The room is comfortable, relaxed, heavily furnished.
Numerous side tables, plants, arm-chairs, book-cabinets, book-
shelves, velvet cloths, a desk, paintings, a large double bed. There
is a large fire in the grate.
The room is lit by a number of table and standard lamps.
LAW *is lying low in an arm-chair, reading, by the fireside.*
Silence.

Exterior. Front area.
STOTT *still.*

Interior. Room.
LAW *in arm-chair. He is smiling at his book.*
He giggles. He is reading a Persian love manual, with illustrations.

Exterior. Front area.
JANE *huddled by the wall.*
STOTT *moves to the door.*

Interior. Room.
Doorbell. LAW *looks up from his book. He closes it, puts it on a side table, goes into the hall.*

Interior. Small hall.
LAW *approaches the front door. He opens it.*
Silence.
He stares at STOTT. *From his position in the doorway* LAW *cannot see the girl.*
LAW (*with great pleasure*). Stott!
STOTT (*smiling*). Hullo, Tim.
LAW. Good God. Come in!

    LAW *laughs.*

  Come in!

    STOTT *enters.*

  I can't believe it!

Interior. Room.
LAW *and* STOTT *enter.*
LAW. Give me your coat. You're soaking. Come on. That's it.
  I'm absolutely flabbergasted. You must be freezing.
STOTT. I am a bit.
LAW. Go on, warm yourself. Warm yourself by the fire.

STOTT. Thanks.

LAW. Sit down by the fire. Go on.

STOTT *moves to the fire.*

LAW *takes the coat into hall.*

Interior. Hall.

LAW *comes into the hall, shaking the raincoat. He looks inside it, at the label, smiles. He hangs it on a hook.*

Interior. Room.

STOTT *warming his hands at the fire.* LAW *comes in.*

LAW. You haven't changed at all. You haven't changed . . . at all!

STOTT *laughs.*

You've got a new raincoat though. Oh yes, I noticed. Hold on, I'll get you a towel.

LAW *goes to the bathroom.*

STOTT, *alone, looks up and about him at the room.*

Interior. Room.
The room.

Interior. Bathroom.

LAW *in bathroom, at the airing cupboard. He swiftly throws aside a number of towels, chooses a soft one with a floral pattern.*

Interior. Room.

LAW *comes in with a towel.*

LAW. Here's a towel. Go on, give it a good wipe. That's it.

You didn't walk here, did you? You're soaking. What happened to your car? You could have driven here. Why didn't you give me a ring? But how did you know my address? My God, it's years. If you'd have rung I would have picked you up. I would have picked you up in my car. What happened to your car?

    STOTT *finishes drying his hair, puts the towel on the arm of a chair.*

STOTT. I got rid of it.

LAW. But how are you? Are you well? You look well.

STOTT. How are you?

LAW. Oh, I'm well. Just a minute, I'll get you some slippers.

    LAW *goes to the cupboard, bends.*

You're going to stay the night, aren't you? You'll have to, look at the time. I wondered if you'd ever turn up again. Really. For years. Here you are. Here's some slippers.

STOTT. Thanks.

    STOTT *takes the slippers, changes his shoes.*

LAW. I'll find some pyjamas in a minute. Still, we'll have a cup of coffee first, or some . . . Or a drink? What about a drink?

STOTT. Ah.

    LAW *pours drinks, brings the drinks to the sofa and sits down by* STOTT.

LAW. You're not living at Chatsworth Road any more, are you? I know that. I've passed by there, numbers of times. You've moved. Where are you living now?

STOTT. I'm looking for a place.

LAW. Stay here! Stay here as long as you like. I've got another bed I can fit up. I've got a camp bed I can fit up.

STOTT. I don't want to impose upon you.

LAW. Not a bit, not a bit.

    Pause.

STOTT. Oh, by the way, I've got a friend outside. Can she come in?

LAW. A friend?

STOTT. Outside.

LAW. A friend? Outside?

STOTT. Can she come in?

LAW. Come in? Yes . . . yes . . . of course . . .

    STOTT *goes towards the door.*

  What's she doing outside?

Exterior. Front door.
JANE *is standing in the narrow porch outside the door.*
The door opens.

Interior. Room.

LAW. STOTT *brings the girl in.*

STOTT. This is Jane. This is Tim Law.

    She smiles.

JANE. It's kind of you.

LAW. How do you do? I . . . must get you a towel.

JANE. No, thank you. My hair was covered.

LAW. But your face?

    STOTT *comes forward.*

STOTT. It's very kind of you, Tim. It really is. Here's a towel.
  (*He gives it to her.*) Here.

LAW. But that's your towel.

JANE. I don't mind, really.

LAW. I have clean ones, dry ones.

JANE (*patting her face*). This is clean.

LAW. But it's not dry.

JANE. It's very soft.

LAW. I have others.

JANE. There. I'm dry.

LAW. You can't be.

JANE. What a splendid room.

STOTT. Isn't it? A little bright, perhaps.

LAW. Too much light?

STOTT turns a lamp off.

STOTT. Do you mind?

LAW. No.

JANE begins to take her clothes off.

In the background STOTT moves about the room, turning off the lamps.

LAW stands still.

STOTT turns off all the lamps but one, by the fireside.

JANE, naked, gets into the bed.

Can I get you some cocoa? Some hot chocolate?

STOTT takes his clothes off and, naked, gets into the bed.

I was feeling quite lonely, actually. It is lonely sitting here, night after night. Mind you, I'm very happy here. Remember that place we shared? That awful place in Chatsworth Road? I've come a long way since then. I bought this flat cash down. It's mine. I don't suppose you've noticed the hi-fi stereo? There's all sorts of things I can show you.

LAW unbuttons his cardigan.

He places it over the one lit lamp, so shading the light. He sits by the fire.

The lamp covered by the cardigan.

Patch of light on the ceiling.

Patch of light at LAW'S feet.

LAW'S hands on the chair arms.

A gasp from JANE.

LAW'S hands do not move.

LAW'S *legs. Beyond them, the fire almost dead.*

LAW *puts on his glasses.*

LAW *reaches for* The Persian Manual of Love.

LAW *peers to read.*
A long sigh from JANE.
LAW *reads.*

Exterior. Cliff-top. Day. Summer.
Long-shot of STOTT *standing on a cliff-top.*

Exterior. Beach.
The beach is long and deserted. LAW *and* JANE, *in swimming*
costumes. JANE *building a sandcastle.* LAW *watches her.*
LAW. How old are you?
JANE. I'm very young.
LAW. You are young.
    He watches her work.
  You're a child.
    He watches her.
  Have you known him long?
JANE. No.
LAW. I have. Charming man. Man of great gifts. Very old
  friend of mine, as a matter of fact. Has he told you?
JANE. No.
LAW. You don't know him very well?

JANE. No.

LAW. He has a connexion with the French aristocracy. He was educated in France. Speaks French fluently, of course. Have you read his French translations?

JANE. No.

LAW. Ah. They're immaculate. Great distinction. Formidable scholar, Stott. Do you know what he got at Oxford? He got a First in Sanskrit at Oxford. A First in Sanskrit!

JANE. How wonderful.

LAW. You never knew?

JANE. Never.

LAW. I know for a fact he owns three chateâux. Three superb châteaux. Have you ever ridden in his Alvis? His Facel Vega? What an immaculate driver. Have you seen his yachts? Huh! What yachts. What yachts.

> JANE *completes her sandcastle.*

How pleased I was to see him. After so long. One loses touch . . . so easily.

Interior. Cave. Day.
STOTT'S *body lying in the sand, asleep.*
LAW *and* JANE *appear at the mouth of the cave. They arrive at the body, look down.*
LAW. What repose he has.
STOTT'S *body in the sand.*
Their shadows across him.

Interior. Room. Night.
LAW *lying on the floor, a cushion at his head, covered by a blanket.*
His eyes are closed.
Silence.
A long gasp from JANE.
LAW'S *eyes open.*

STOTT *and* JANE *in bed.*
STOTT *turning to wall.*
JANE *turns to the edge of the bed.*
She leans over the edge of the bed and smiles at LAW.

LAW *looks at her.*

JANE *smiles.*

Interior. Room. Day.
STOTT *lifts a painting from the wall, looks at it.*
STOTT. No.
LAW. No, you're quite right. I've never liked it.
  STOTT *walks across room to a second picture, looks at it. He*
  turns to look at LAW.
No.
  STOTT *takes it down and turns to look at the other paintings.*
All of them. All of them. You're right. They're terrible. Take
them down.
  The paintings are all similar watercolours.
  STOTT *begins to take them from the walls.*

Interior. Kitchen. Day.
JANE *in the kitchen, cooking at the stove, humming.*

Exterior. Backyard. Winter. Day.
The yard is surrounded by high blank walls.

STOTT *and* LAW *sitting at an iron table, with a pole for an umbrella.*

They are drinking lager.

LAW. Who is she? Where did you meet her?

STOTT. She's charming, isn't she?

LAW. Charming. A little young.

STOTT. She comes from a rather splendid family, actually.

LAW. Really?

STOTT. Rather splendid.

> *Pause.*

LAW. Very helpful, of course, around the house.

STOTT. Plays the harp, you know.

LAW. Well?

STOTT. Remarkably well.

LAW. What a pity I don't possess one. You don't possess a harp, do you?

STOTT. Of course I possess a harp.

LAW. A recent acquisition?

STOTT. No, I've had it for years.

> *Pause.*

LAW. You don't find she's lacking in maturity?

Exterior. Beach. Summer. Day.

LAW *and* JANE *lying in the sand.* JANE *caressing him.*

JANE (*whispering*). Yes, yes, yes, oh you are, oh you are, oh you are . . .

LAW. We can be seen.

JANE. Why do you resist? How can you resist?

LAW. We can be seen! Damn you!

Exterior. Backyard. Winter. Day.

STOTT *and* LAW *at the table with lager.*

JANE *comes to the back door.*

IANE. Lunch is up!

Interior. Hall. Day.
LAW *and* JANE *come in at the front door with towels over their shoulders.*

Interior. Room. Day. Summer.
LAW *and* JANE *at the entrance of the room, towels over their shoulders, staring at the room.*
The room is unrecognizable. The furnishing has changed. There are Scandinavian tables and desks. Large bowls of Swedish glass. Tubular chairs. An Indian rug. Parquet floors, shining. A new hi-fi cabinet, etc. Fireplace blocked. The bed is the same.
STOTT *is at the window, closing the curtains. He turns.*
STOTT. Have a good swim?

Interior. Room. Night. Winter. (Second furnishing.)
STOTT *and* JANE *in bed, smoking.* LAW *sitting.*
STOTT. Let's have some music. We haven't heard your hi-fi for ages. Let's hear your stereo. What are you going to play?

Interior. Bar. Evening.
Large empty bar. All the tables unoccupied.
STOTT, LAW *and* JANE *at one table.*
STOTT. This was one of our old haunts, wasn't it, Tim? This was one of our haunts. Tim was always my greatest friend, you know. Always. It's marvellous. I've found my old friend again –
    Looking at JANE.
And discovered a new. And you like each other so much. It's really very warming.
LAW. Same again? (*To* WAITER.) Same again. (*To* JANE.)

Same again? (*To* WAITER.) Same again. The same again, all round. Exactly the same.

STOTT. I'll change to Campari.

LAW (*clicking his fingers at the* WAITER). One Campari here. Otherwise the same again.

STOTT. Remember those nights reading Proust? Remember them?

LAW (*to* JANE). In the original.

STOTT. The bouts with Laforgue? What bouts.

LAW. I remember.

STOTT. The great elms they had then. The great elm trees.

LAW. And the poplars.

STOTT. The cricket. The squash courts. You were pretty hot stuff at squash, you know.

LAW. You were unbeatable.

STOTT. Your style was deceptive.

LAW. It still is.

> LAW *laughs.*

It still is!

STOTT. Not any longer.

> *The* WAITER *serves the drinks.*
> *Silence.* STOTT *lifts his glass.*

Yes, I really am a happy man.

Exterior. Field. Evening. Winter.

STOTT *and* LAW. JANE *one hundred yards across the field.*

She holds a scarf.

LAW (*shouting*). Hold the scarf up. When you drop it, we run.

> *She holds the scarf up.*
> LAW *rubs his hands.* STOTT *looks at him.*

STOTT. Are you quite sure you want to do this?

LAW. Of course I'm sure.

JANE. On your marks!

> STOTT *and* LAW *get on their marks.*

Get set!
>*They get set.*
>JANE *drops scarf.*

Go!
>LAW *runs.* STOTT *stays still.*
>LAW, *going fast, turns to look for* STOTT; *off balance, stumbles, falls, hits his chin on the ground.*
>*Lying flat, he looks back at* STOTT.

LAW. Why didn't you run?

Exterior. Field.
JANE *stands, scarf in her hand. Downfield,* STOTT *stands.*
LAW *lies on the grass.* LAW'S *voice:*
LAW. Why didn't you run?

Interior. Room. Night. Winter. (Second furnishing.)
STOTT. Let's have some music. We haven't heard your hi-fi for ages.
>STOTT *opens the curtains and the window.*
>*Moonlight.* LAW *and* JANE *sit in chairs, clench their bodies with cold.*

Exterior. Backyard. Day. Winter.
STOTT *walking.* LAW, *wearing a heavy overcoat, collar turned up, watching him.* LAW *approaches him.*
LAW. Listen. Listen. I must speak to you. I must speak frankly. Listen. Don't you think it's a bit crowded in that flat, for the three of us?
STOTT. No, no. Not at all.
LAW. Listen, listen. Stop walking. Stop walking. Please. Wait.
>STOTT *stops.*

Listen. Wouldn't you say that the flat is a little small, for three people?

STOTT (*patting his shoulder*). No, no. Not at all.

STOTT *continues walking.*

LAW (*following him*). To look at it another way, to look at it another way, I can assure you that the Council would object strenuously to three people living in these conditions. The Town Council, I know for a fact, would feel it incumbent upon itself to register the strongest possible objections. And so would the Church.

STOTT *stops walking, looks at him.*

STOTT. Not at all. Not at all.

Interior. Room. Day. Summer.
The curtains are closed. The three at lunch, at the table. STOTT *and* JANE *are wearing tropical clothes.* JANE *is sitting on* STOTT'S *lap.*

LAW. Why don't we open the curtains?

STOTT *eats a grape.*

It's terribly close. Shall I open the window?

STOTT. What are you going to play? Debussy, I hope.

LAW *goes to the record cabinet. He examines record after record, feverishly, flings them one after the other at the wall.*

STOTT. Where's Debussy?

STOTT *kisses* JANE.

Another record hits the wall.

Where's Debussy? That's what we want. That's what we need. That's what we need at the moment.

JANE *breaks away from* STOTT *and goes out into the yard.*

STOTT *sits still.*

LAW. I've found it!

Interior. Room. Night. Winter.
LAW *turns with the record.*

The room is furnished as at the beginning.
STOTT *and* JANE, *naked, climb into bed.*
LAW *puts the record down and places his cardigan over the one lit lamp.*
He sits, picks up the poker and pokes the dying fire.

Exterior. Backyard. Day. Summer.
JANE *sitting at the iron table.*
STOTT *approaches her with a glass and bottle.*
He pours wine into the glass.
He bends over her, attempts to touch her breast.
She moves her body away from him.
STOTT *remains still.*

LAW *watches from the open windows.*
He moves to the table with the record and smiles at STOTT.
LAW. I've found the record. The music you wanted.
    STOTT *slams his glass on the table and goes into the room.*
    LAW *sits at the table, drinks from the bottle, regards* JANE.
    JANE *plays with a curl in her hair.*

Interior. Cave by the sea. Evening. Summer.
LAW *and* JANE. *He lying, she sitting, by him.*
She bends and whispers to him.
JANE. Why don't you tell him to go? We had such a lovely home. We had such a cosy home. It was so warm. Tell him to go. It's your place. Then we could be happy again. Like we used to. Like we used to. In our first blush of love. Then we could be happy again, like we used to. We could be happy again. Like we used to.

Exterior. Backyard. Night. Winter.
The yard is icy. The window is open. The room is lit.
LAW *is whispering to* STOTT *at the window. In the background*
JANE *sits sewing.* (*Second furnishing.*)

Exterior. Backyard. Window.
LAW *and* STOTT *at the open window,* STOTT'S *body hunched.*
LAW (*whispering very deliberately*). She betrays you. She betrays
    you. She has no loyalty. After all you've done for her. Shown
    her the world. Given her faith. You've been deluded. She's
    a savage. A viper. She sullies this room. She dirties this
    room. All this beautiful furniture. This beautiful Scandi-
    navian furniture. She dirties it. She sullies the room.
        STOTT *turns slowly to regard* JANE.

Interior. Room. Day.
The curtains are closed.
STOTT *in bed.* JANE *bending over him, touching his head.*
She looks across at LAW.
Silence. (*Second furnishing.*)
LAW. Is he breathing?
JANE. Just.
LAW. His last, do you think?
    Pause.
  Do you think it could be his last?
JANE. It could be.
LAW. How could it have happened? He seemed so fit. He was
    fit. As fit as a fiddle. Perhaps we should have called a doctor.
    And now he's dying. Are you heartbroken?
JANE. Yes.
LAW. So am I.
    Pause.
JANE. What shall we do with the body?

LAW. Body? He's not dead yet. Perhaps he'll recover.
  They stare at each other.

Interior. Room. Night.
LAW *and* JANE *in a corner, snuffling each other like animals.*

Interior. Room. Night.
STOTT *at the window. He opens the curtains. Moonlight pierces the room. He looks round.*

Interior. Room. Night.
LAW *and* JANE *in a corner, looking up at the window, blinking.*

Interior. Room. Day.
STOTT *at the window, closing the curtains. He turns into the room. The room is unrecognizable. The walls are hung with tapestries, an oval Florentine mirror, an oblong Italian Master. The floor is marble tiles. There are marble pillars with hanging plants, carved golden chairs, a rich carpet along the room's centre.*
STOTT *sits in a chair.* JANE *comes forward with a bowl of fruit.*
STOTT *chooses a grape. In the background* LAW, *in a corner, playing the flute.* STOTT *bites into the grape, tosses the bowl of fruit across the room. The fruit scatters.* JANE *rushes to collect it.*
STOTT *picks up a tray containing large marbles.*
He rolls the tray. The marbles knock against each other.
He selects a marble. He looks across the room at LAW *playing the flute.*

LAW *with flute.*
At the other end of the room STOTT *prepares to bowl.*
STOTT. Play!

STOTT *bowls.*

The marble crashes into the wall behind LAW.

LAW *stands, takes guard with his flute.*

STOTT. Play!
    STOTT *bowls.*

The marble crashes into the window behind LAW.

LAW *takes guard.*
STOTT. Play!
    STOTT *bowls. The marble hits* LAW *on the knee.*

LAW *hops.*

LAW *takes guard.*

STOTT. Play!
    STOTT *bowls.*

LAW *brilliantly cuts marble straight into golden fish tank. The tank smashes. Dozens of fish swim across the marble tiles.*

JANE, *in the corner, applauds.*

LAW *waves his flute in acknowledgement.*

STOTT. Play!
 STOTT *bowls.*

Marble crashes into LAW'S *forehead. He drops.*

Interior. Kitchen. Night.
JANE *in the kitchen, putting spoonfuls of instant coffee into two cups.*

Interior. Room. Night.
The room is completely bare.
Bare walls. Bare floorboards. No furniture. One hanging bulb.
STOTT *and* LAW *at opposite ends of the room.*
They face each other. They are barefooted. They each hold a broken milk bottle. They are crouched, still.

LAW'S *face, sweating.*

STOTT'S *face, sweating.*

LAW *from* STOTT'S *viewpoint.*

STOTT *from* LAW'S *viewpoint.*

JANE *pouring sugar from a packet into the bowl.*

LAW *pointing his bottle before him, his arm taut.*

STOTT *pointing his bottle before him, his arm taut.*

JANE *pouring milk from a bottle into a jug.*

STOTT *slowly advancing along bare boards.*

LAW *slowly advancing.*

JANE *pouring a small measure of milk into the cups.*

LAW *and* STOTT *drawing closer.*

JANE *putting sugar into the cups.*

The broken milk bottles, in shaking hands, almost touching.

The broken milk bottles fencing, not touching.

JANE *stirring milk, sugar and coffee in the cups.*

The broken milk bottles, in a sudden thrust, smashing together.

Record turning on a turntable. Sudden music.
Debussy's 'Girl With The Flaxen Hair'.

Exterior. Front area. Night.
LAW *standing centre, looking at the basement door.*
JANE *crouched by the wall. Rainhat. Raincoat.* LAW *wearing*
STOTT'S *raincoat.*

Interior. Room.
Furnished as at the beginning.
STOTT *sitting by the fire, reading. He is smiling at his book.*

Exterior. Front area.
LAW *still.*

Interior. Room.
STOTT *turns a page.*
Doorbell.
STOTT *looks up, puts his book down, stands, goes into the hall.*

Interior. Room.
The room still. The fire burning.

Interior. Hall.

STOTT *approaches the front door. He opens it.*

Silence.

He stares at LAW. *From his position in the doorway* STOTT
cannot see JANE.

STOTT (*with great pleasure*). Law!

LAW (*smiling*). Hullo, Charles.

STOTT. Good God. Come in!

    STOTT *laughs.*

Come in!

    LAW *enters.*

I can't believe it!

Landscape

Landscape was first presented on radio by the BBC on 25th April, 1968, with the following cast:

BETH   Peggy Ashcroft
DUFF   Eric Porter

Directed by Guy Vaesen

The play was first presented on the stage by the Royal Shakespeare Company at the Aldwych Theatre on 2nd July, 1969, with the following cast:

BETH   Peggy Ashcroft
DUFF   David Waller

Directed by Peter Hall

DUFF: a man in his early fifties.

BETH: a woman in her late forties.

The kitchen of a country house.

A long kitchen table.

BETH sits in an armchair, which stands away from the table, to its left.

DUFF sits in a chair at the right corner of the table. The background, of a sink, stove, etc., and a window, is dim. Evening.

NOTE:

DUFF *refers normally to* BETH, *but does not appear to hear her voice.*

BETH *never looks at* DUFF, *and does not appear to hear his voice.*

Both characters are relaxed, in no sense rigid.

BETH

I would like to stand by the sea. It is there.

Pause

I have. Many times. It's something I cared for. I've done it.

Pause

I'll stand on the beach. On the beach. Well ... it was very fresh. But it was hot, in the dunes. But it was so fresh, on the shore. I loved it very much.

Pause

Lots of people ...

Pause

People move so easily. Men. Men move.

Pause

I walked from the dune to the shore. My man slept in the dune. He turned over as I stood. His eyelids. Belly button. Snoozing how lovely.

Pause

Would you like a baby? I said. Children? Babies? Of our own? Would be nice.

Pause

Women turn, look at me.

Pause

Our own child? Would you like that?

Pause

Two women looked at me, turned and stared. No. I was walking, they were still. I turned.

Pause

Why do you look?

Pause

I didn't say that, I stared. Then I was looking at them.

Pause

I am beautiful.

Pause

I walked back over the sand. He had turned. Toes under sand, head buried in his arms.

DUFF

The dog's gone. I didn't tell you.

Pause

I had to shelter under a tree for twenty minutes yesterday. Because of the rain. I meant to tell you. With some youngsters. I didn't know them.

Pause

Then it eased. A downfall. I walked up as far as the pond. Then I felt a couple of big drops. Luckily I was only a few yards from the shelter. I sat down in there. I meant to tell you.

Pause

Do you remember the weather yesterday? That downfall.?

BETH

He felt my shadow. He looked up at me standing above him.

DUFF

I should have had some bread with me. I could have fed the birds.

BETH

Sand on his arms.

DUFF

They were hopping about. Making a racket.

BETH

I lay down by him, not touching.

DUFF

There wasn't anyone else in the shelter. There was a man and woman, under the trees, on the other side of the pond. I didn't feel like getting wet. I stayed where I was.

Pause

Yes, I've forgotten something. The dog was with me.

Pause

BETH

Did those women know me? I didn't remember their faces. I'd never seen their faces before. I'd never seen those women before. I'm certain of it. Why were they looking at me? There's nothing strange about me. There's nothing strange about the way I look. I look like anyone.

DUFF

The dog wouldn't have minded me feeding the birds. Anyway, as soon as we got in the shelter he fell asleep. But even if he'd been awake . . . . .

Pause

BETH

They all held my arm lightly, as I stepped out of the car, or
out of the door, or down the steps. Without exception. If
they touched the back of my neck, or my hand, it was done so
lightly. Without exception. With one exception.

DUFF

Mind you, there was a lot of shit all over the place, all along the
paths, by the pond. Dogshit, duckshit . . . all kinds of shit . . .
all over the paths. The rain didn't clean it up. It made it even
more treacherous.

Pause

The ducks were well away, right over on their island. But I
wouldn't have fed them, anyway. I would have fed the
sparrows.

BETH

I could stand now. I could be the same. I dress differently, but
I am beautiful.

Silence

DUFF

You should have a walk with me one day down to the pond,
bring some bread. There's nothing to stop you.

Pause

I sometimes run into one or two people I know. You might
remember them.

Pause

BETH

When I watered the flowers he stood, watching me, and watched
me arrange them. My gravity, he said. I was so grave, attending

to the flowers, I'm going to water and arrange the flowers, I said. He followed me and watched, standing at a distance from me. When the arrangement was done I stayed still. I heard him moving. He didn't touch me. I listened. I looked at the flowers, blue and white, in the bowl.

Pause

Then he touched me.

Pause

He touched the back of my neck. His fingers, lightly, touching, lightly, touching, the back, of my neck.

DUFF

The funny thing was, when I looked, when the shower was over, the man and woman under the trees on the other side of the pond had gone. There wasn't a soul in the park.

BETH

I wore a white beach robe. Underneath I was naked.

Pause

There wasn't a soul on the beach. Very far away a man was sitting, on a breakwater. But even so he was only a pinpoint, in the sun. And even so I could only see him when I was standing, or on my way from the shore to the dune. When I lay down I could no longer see him, therefore he couldn't see me.

Pause

I may have been mistaken. Perhaps the beach was empty. Perhaps there was no-one there.

Pause

He couldn't see .. my man .. anyway. He never stood up.

Pause

Snoozing how lovely I said to him. But I wasn't a fool, on that occasion. I lay quiet, by his side.

Silence

DUFF

Anyway . . .

BETH

My skin . . .

DUFF

I'm sleeping all right these days.

BETH

Was stinging.

DUFF

Right through the night, every night.

BETH

I'd been in the sea.

DUFF

Maybe it's something to do with the fishing. Getting to learn more about fish.

BETH

Stinging in the sea by myself.

DUFF

They're very shy creatures. You've got to woo them. You must never get excited with them. Or flurried. Never.

BETH

I knew there must be a hotel near, where we could get some
tea.

Silence

DUFF

Anyway . . . luck was on my side for a change. By the time I
got out of the park the pubs were open.

Pause

So I thought I might as well pop in and have a pint. I wanted
to tell you. I met some nut in there. First of all I had a word
with the landlord. He knows me. Then this nut came in. He
ordered a pint and he made a criticism of the beer. I had no
patience with it.

BETH

But then I thought perhaps the hotel bar will be open. We'll
sit in the bar. He'll buy me a drink. What will I order? But
what will he order? What will he want? I shall hear him say
it. I shall hear his voice. He will ask me what I would like
first. Then he'll order the two drinks. I shall hear him do it.

DUFF

This beer is piss, he said. Undrinkable. There's nothing wrong
with the beer, I said. Yes there is, he said, I just told you what
was wrong with it. It's the best beer in the area, I said. No it
isn't, this chap said, it's piss. The landlord picked up the mug
and had a sip. Good beer, he said. Someone's made a mistake,
this fellow said, someone's used this pintpot instead of the
boghole.

Pause

The landlord threw a half a crown on the bar and told him to take it. The pint's only two and three, the man said, I owe you three pence, but I haven't got any change. Give the threepence to your son, the landlord said, with my compliments. I haven't got a son, the man said, I've never had any children. I bet you're not even married, the landlord said. This man said: I'm not married. No-one'll marry me.

Pause

Then the man asked the landlord and me if we would have a drink with him. The landlord said he'd have a pint. I didn't answer at first, but the man came over to me and said: Have one with *me*. Have one with *me*.

Pause

He put down a ten bob note and said he'd have a pint as well.

Silence

BETH

Suddenly I stood. I walked to the shore and into the water. I didn't swim. I don't swim. I let the water billow me. I rested in the water. The waves were very light, delicate. They touched the back of my neck.

Silence

DUFF

One day when the weather's good you could go out into the garden and sit down. You'd like that. The open air. I'm often out there. The dog liked it.

Pause

I've put in some flowers. You'd find it pleasant. Looking at the flowers. You could cut a few if you liked. Bring them in. No-one would see you. There's no-one there.

Pause

That's where we're lucky, in my opinion. To live in Mr Sykes'
house in peace, no-one to bother us. I've thought of inviting
one or two people I know from the village in here for a bit of
a drink once or twice but I decided against it. It's not necessary.

Pause

You know what you get quite a lot of out in the garden?
Butterflies.

BETH

I slipped out of my costume and put on my beachrobe. Underneath I was naked. There wasn't a soul on the beach. Except
for an elderly man, far away on a breakwater. I lay down
beside him and whispered. Would you like a baby? A child?
Of our own? Would be nice.

Pause

DUFF

What did you think of that downfall?

Pause

Of course the youngsters I met under the first tree, during the
first shower, they were larking about and laughing. I tried to
listen, to find out what they were laughing about, but I
couldn't work it out. They were whispering. I tried to listen,
to find out what the joke was.

Pause

Anyway I didn't find out.

Pause

I was thinking ... when you were young ... you didn't laugh much. You were ... grave.

Silence

BETH

That's why he'd picked such a desolate place. So that I could draw in peace. I had my sketch book with me. I took it out. I took my drawing pencil out. But there was nothing to draw. Only the beach, the sea.

Pause

Could have drawn him. He didn't want it. He laughed.

Pause

I laughed, with him.

Pause

I waited for him to laugh, then I would smile, turn away, he would touch my back, turn me, to him. My nose .. creased. I would laugh with him, a little.

Pause

He laughed. I'm sure of it. So I didn't draw him.

Silence

DUFF

You were a first-rate housekeeper when you were young. Weren't you? I was very proud. You never made a fuss, you never got into a state, you went about your work. He could rely on you. He did. He trusted you, to run his house, to keep the house up to the mark, no panic.

Pause

Do you remember when I took him on that trip to the north? That long trip. When we got back he thanked you for looking after the place so well, everything running like clockwork.

Pause

You'd missed me. When I came into this room you stopped still. I had to walk all the way over the floor towards you.

Pause

I touched you.

Pause

But I had something to say to you, didn't I? I waited, I didn't say it then, but I'd made up my mind to say it, I'd decided I would say it, and I did say it, the next morning. Didn't I?

Pause

I told you that I'd let you down. I'd been unfaithful to you.

Pause

You didn't cry. We had a few hours off. We walked up to the pond, with the dog. We stood under the trees for a bit. I didn't know why you'd brought that carrier bag with you. I asked you. I said what's in that bag? It turned out to be bread. You fed the ducks. Then we stood under the trees and looked across the pond.

Pause

When we got back into this room you put your hands on my face and you kissed me.

BETH

But I didn't really want a drink.

Pause

I drew a face in the sand, then a body. The body of a woman. Then the body of a man, close to her, not touching. But they didn't look like anything. They didn't look like human figures. The sand kept on slipping, mixing the contours. I crept close to him and put my head on his arm, and closed my eyes. All those darting red and black flecks, under my eyelid. I moved my cheek on his skin. And all those darting red and black flecks, moving about under my eyelid. I buried my face in his side and shut the light out.

Silence

DUFF

Mr Sykes took to us from the very first interview, didn't he?

Pause

He said I've got the feeling you'll make a very good team. Do you remember? And that's what we proved to be. No question. I could drive well, I could polish his shoes well, I earned my keep. Turn my hand to anything. He never lacked for anything, in the way of being looked after. Mind you, he was a gloomy bugger.

Pause

I was never sorry for him, at any time, for his lonely life.

Pause

That nice blue dress he chose for you, for the house, that was very nice of him. Of course it was in his own interests for you to look good about the house, for guests.

BETH

He moved in the sand and put his arm around me.

Silence

DUFF

Do you like me to talk to you?

Pause

Do you like me to tell you about all the things I've been doing?

Pause

About all the things I've been thinking?

Pause

Mmmnn?

Pause

I think you do.

BETH

And cuddled me.

Silence

DUFF

Of course it was in his own interests to see that you were attractively dressed about the house, to give a good impression to his guests.

BETH

I caught a bus to the crossroads and then walked down the lane by the old church. It was very quiet, except for birds. There was an old man fiddling about on the cricket pitch, bending. I stood out of the sun, under a tree.

Pause

I heard the car. He saw me and stopped me. I stayed still. Then the car moved again, came towards me slowly. I moved round the front of it, in the dust. I couldn't see him for the

sun, but he was watching me. When I got to the door it was
locked. I looked through at him. He leaned over and opened
the door. I got in and sat beside him. He smiled at me. Then
he reversed, all in one movement, very quickly, quite straight,
up the lane to the crossroads, and we drove to the sea.

Pause

DUFF

We're the envy of a lot of people, you know, living in this
house, having this house all to ourselves. It's too big for two
people.

BETH

He said he knew a very desolate beach, that no-one else in the
world knew, and that's where we are going.

DUFF

I was very gentle to you. I was kind to you, that day. I knew
you'd had a shock, so I was gentle with you. I held your arm
on the way back from the pond. You put your hands on my
face and kissed me.

BETH

All the food I had in my bag I had cooked myself, or prepared
myself. I had baked the bread myself.

DUFF

The girl herself I considered unimportant. I didn't think it
necessary to go into details. I decided against it.

BETH

The windows were open but we kept the hood up.

Pause

DUFF

Mr Sykes gave a little dinner party that Friday. He compli-
mented you on your cooking and the service.

Pause

Two women. That was all. Never seen them before. Probably
his mother and sister.

Pause

They wanted coffee late. I was in bed. I fell asleep. I would
have come down to the kitchen to give you a hand but I was
too tired.

Pause

But I woke up when you got into bed. You were out on your
feet. You were asleep as soon as you hit the pillow. Your body
. . . just fell back.

BETH

He was right. It was desolate. There wasn't a soul on the
beach.

Silence

DUFF

I had a look over the house the other day. I meant to tell you.
The dust is bad. We'll have to polish it up.

Pause

We could go up to the drawing room, open the windows. I
could wash the old decanters. We could have a drink up there
one evening, if it's a pleasant evening.

Pause

I think there's moths. I moved the curtain and they flew out.

Pause

BETH

Of course when I'm older I won't be the same as I am, I won't be what I am, my skirts, my long legs, I'll be older, I won't be the same.

DUFF

At least now ... at least now, I can walk down to the pub in peace and up to the pond in peace, with no-one to nag the shit out of me.

Silence

BETH

All it is, you see ... I said ... is the lightness of your touch, the lightness of your look, my neck, your eyes, the silence, that is my meaning, the loveliness of my flowers, my hands touching my flowers, that is my meaning.

Pause

I've watched other people. I've seen them.

Pause

All the cars zooming by. Men with girls at their sides. Bouncing up and down. They're dolls. They squeak.

Pause

All the people were squeaking in the hotel bar. The girls had long hair. They were smiling.

DUFF

That's what matters, anyway. We're together. That's what matters.

Silence

BETH

But I was up early. There was still plenty to be done and cleared up. I had put the plates in the sink to soak. They had soaked overnight. They were easy to wash. The dog was up. He followed me. Misty morning. Comes from the river.

DUFF

This fellow knew bugger all about beer. He didn't know I'd been trained as a cellarman. That's why I could speak with authority.

BETH

I opened the door and went out. There was no-one about. The sun was shining. Wet, I mean wetness, all over the ground.

DUFF

A cellarman is the man responsible. He's the earliest up in the morning. Give the drayman a hand with the barrels. Down the slide through the cellarflaps. Lower them by rope to the racks. Rock them on the belly, put a rim up them, use balance and leverage, hike them up onto the racks.

BETH

Still misty, but thinner, thinning.

DUFF

The bung is on the vertical, in the bunghole. Spile the bung. Hammer the spile through the centre of the bung. That lets the air through the bung, down the bunghole, lets the beer breathe.

BETH

Wetness all over the air. Sunny. Trees like feathers.

DUFF

Then you hammer the tap in.

BETH

I wore my blue dress.

DUFF

Let it stand for three days. Keep wet sacks over the barrels. Hose the cellar floor daily. Hose the barrels daily.

BETH

It was a beautiful autumn morning.

DUFF

Run water through the pipes to the bar pumps daily.

BETH

I stood in the mist.

DUFF

Pull off. Pull off. Stop pulling just before you get to the dregs. The dregs'll give you the shits. You've got an ullage barrel. Feed the slops back to the ullage barrel, send them back to the brewery.

BETH

In the sun.

DUFF

Dip the barrels daily with a brass rod. Know your gallonage. Chalk it up. Then you're tidy. Then you never get caught short.

BETH

Then I went back to the kitchen and sat down.

Pause

DUFF

This chap in the pub said he was surprised to hear it. He said he was surprised to hear about hosing the cellar floor. He said he thought most cellars had a thermostatically controlled cooling system. He said he thought keg beer was fed with oxygen through a cylinder. I said I wasn't talking about keg beer, I was talking about normal draught beer. He said he thought they piped the beer from a tanker into metal containers. I said they may do, but he wasn't talking about the quality of beer I was. He accepted that point.

Pause

BETH

The dog sat down by me. I stroked him. Through the window I could see down into the valley. I saw children in the valley. They were running through the grass. They ran up the hill.

Long Silence

DUFF

I never saw your face. You were standing by the windows. One of those black nights. A downfall. All I could hear was the rain on the glass, smacking on the glass. You knew I'd come in but you didn't move. I stood close to you. What were you looking at? It was black outside. I could just see your shape in the window, your reflection. There must have been some kind of light somewhere. Perhaps just your face reflected, lighter than all the rest. I stood close to you. Perhaps you were just thinking, in a dream. Without touching you, I could feel your bottom.

Silence

BETH

I remembered always, in drawing, the basic principles of

shadow and light. Objects intercepting the light cast shadows. Shadow is deprivation of light. The shape of the shadow is determined by that of the object. But not always. Not always directly. Sometimes it is only indirectly affected by it. Sometimes the cause of the shadow cannot be found.

Pause

But I always bore in mind the basic principles of drawing.

Pause

So that I never lost track. Or heart.

Pause

DUFF

You used to wear a chain round your waist. On the chain you carried your keys, your thimble, your notebook, your pencil, your scissors.

Pause

You stood in the hall and banged the gong.

Pause

What the bloody hell are you doing banging that bloody gong?

Pause

It's bullshit. Standing in an empty hall banging a bloody gong. There's no one to listen. No one'll hear. There's not a soul in the house. Except me. There's nothing for lunch. There's nothing cooked. No stew. No pie. No greens. No joint. Fuck all.

Pause

BETH

So that I never lost track. Even though, even when, I asked

him to turn, to look at me, but he turned to look at me but I couldn't see his look.

Pause

I couldn't see whether he was looking at me.

Pause

Although he had turned. And appeared to be looking at me.

DUFF

I took the chain off and the thimble, the keys, the scissors slid off it and clattered down. I booted the gong down the hall. The dog came in. I thought you would come to me, I thought you would come into my arms and kiss me, even ... offer yourself to me. I would have had you in front of the dog, like a man, in the hall, on the stone, banging the gong, mind you don't get the scissors up your arse, or the thimble, don't worry, I'll throw them for the dog to chase, the thimble will keep the dog happy, he'll play with it with his paws, you'll plead with me like a woman, I'll bang the gong on the floor, if the sound is too flat, lacks resonance, I'll hang it back on its hook, bang you against it swinging, gonging, waking the place up, calling them all for dinner, lunch is up, bring out the bacon, bang your lovely head, mind the dog doesn't swallow the thimble, slam—

Silence

BETH

He lay above me and looked down at me. He supported my shoulder.

Pause

So tender his touch on my neck. So softly his kiss on my cheek.

Pause

My hand on his rib.

Pause

So sweetly the sand over me. Tiny the sand on my skin.

Pause

So silent the sky in my eyes. Gently the sound of the tide.

Pause

Oh my true love I said.

Silence

Silence was first presented by the Royal Shakespeare Company at the Aldwych Theatre on 2nd July, 1969, with the following cast:

ELLEN: a girl in her twenties   Frances Cuka
RUMSEY: a man of forty   Anthony Bate
BATES: a man in his middle thirties   Norman Rodway
                    Directed by Peter Hall

Three areas.
A chair in each area.

RUMSEY

I walk with my girl who wears a grey blouse when she walks and grey shoes and walks with me readily wearing her clothes considered for me. Her grey clothes.

She holds my arm.

On good evenings we walk through the hills to the top of the hill past the dogs the clouds racing just before dark or as dark is falling when the moon

When it's chilly I stop her and slip her raincoat over her shoulders or rainy slip arms into the arms, she twisting her arms. And talk to her and tell her everything.

She dresses for my eyes.

I tell her my thoughts. Now I am ready to walk, her arm in me her hand in me.

I tell her my life's thoughts, clouds racing. She looks up at me or listens looking down. She stops in midsentence, my sentence, to look up at me. Sometimes her hand has slipped from mine, her arm loosened, she walks slightly apart, dog barks.

ELLEN

There are two. One who is with me sometimes, and another. He listens to me. I tell him what I know. We walk by the dogs.

Sometimes the wind is so high he does not hear me. I lead him to a tree, clasp closely to him and whisper to him, wind going, dogs stop, and he hears me.

But the other hears me.

BATES

Caught a bus to the town. Crowds. Lights round the market, rain and stinking. Showed her the bumping lights. Took her down around the dumps. Black roads and girders. She clutching me. This way the way I bring you. Pubs throw the doors smack into the night. Cars barking and the lights. She with me, clutching.

Brought her into this place, my cousin runs it. Undressed her, placed my hand.

ELLEN

I go by myself with the milk to the top, the clouds racing, all the blue changes, I'm dizzy sometimes, meet with him under some place.

One time visited his house. He put a light on, it reflected the window, it reflected in the window.

RUMSEY

She walks from the door to the window to see the way she has come, to confirm that the house which grew nearer is the same one she stands in, that the path and the bushes are the same, that the gate is the same. When I stand beside her and smile at her, she looks at me and smiles.

BATES

How many times standing clenched in the pissing dark waiting?

The mud, the cows, the river.

You cross the field out of darkness. You arrive.

You stand breathing before me. You smile.

I put my hands on your shoulders and press. Press the smile off your face.

ELLEN

There are two. I turn to them and speak. I look them in their eyes. I kiss them there and say, I look away to smile, and touch them as I turn.

Silence

RUMSEY

I watch the clouds. Pleasant the ribs and tendons of cloud.

I've lost nothing.

Pleasant alone and watch the folding light. My animals are quiet. My heart never bangs. I read in the evenings. There is no-one to tell me what is expected or not expected of me. There is nothing required of me.

BATES

I'm at my last gasp with this unendurable racket. I kicked open the door and stood before them. Someone called me Grandad and told me to button it. It's they should button it. Were I young . . .

One of them told me I was lucky to be alive, that I would have to bear it in order to pay for being alive, in order to give thanks for being alive.

It's a question of sleep. I need something of it, or how can I remain alive, without any true rest, having no solace, no constant solace, not even any damn inconstant solace.

I am strong, but not as strong as the bastards in the other room, and their tittering bitches, and their music, and their love.

If I changed my life, perhaps, and lived deliberately at night, and slept in the day. But what exactly would I do? What can be meant by living in the dark?

ELLEN

Now and again I meet my drinking companion and have a drink with her. She is a friendly woman, quite elderly, quite friendly. But she knows little of me, she could never know much of me, not really, not now. She's funny. She starts talking sexily to me, in the corner, with our drinks. I laugh.

She asks me about my early life, when I was young, never departing from her chosen subject, but I have nothing to tell her about the sexual part of my youth. I'm old, I tell her, my youth was somewhere else, anyway I don't remember. She does the talking anyway.

I like to get back to my room. It has a pleasant view. I have one or two friends, ladies. They ask me where I come from. I say of course from the country. I don't see much of them.

I sometimes wonder if I think. I heard somewhere about how many thoughts go through the brain of a person. But I couldn't remember anything I'd actually thought, for some time.

It isn't something that anyone could ever tell me, could ever reassure me about, nobody could tell, from looking at me, what was happening.

But I'm still quite pretty really, quite nice eyes, nice skin.

BATES *moves to* ELLEN

BATES

Will we meet to-night?

ELLEN

I don't know.

Pause

BATES

Come with me to-night.

ELLEN

Where?

BATES

Anywhere. For a walk.

Pause

ELLEN

I don't want to walk.

BATES

Why not?

Pause

ELLEN

I want to go somewhere else.

Pause

BATES

Where?

ELLEN

I don't know.

Pause

BATES

What's wrong with a walk?

ELLEN

I don't want to walk.

Pause

BATES

What do you want to do?

ELLEN

I don't know.

Pause

BATES

Do you want to go anywhere else?

ELLEN

Yes.

BATES

Where?

ELLEN

I don't know.

Pause

BATES

Do you want me to buy you a drink?

ELLEN

No.

Pause

BATES

Come for a walk.

ELLEN

No.

Pause

BATES

All right. I'll take you on a bus to the town. I know a place. My cousin runs it.

ELLEN

No.

Silence

RUMSEY

It is curiously hot. Sitting weather, I call it. The weather sits, does not move. Unusual. I shall walk down to my horse and see how my horse is. He'll come towards me.

Perhaps he doesn't need me. My visit, my care, will be like any other visit, any other care. I can't believe it.

BATES

I walk in my mind. But can't get out of the walls, into a wind.

Meadows are walled, and lakes. The sky's a wall.

Once I had a little girl. I took it for walks. I held it by its hand. It looked up at me and said, I see something in a tree, a shape, a shadow. It is leaning down. It is looking at us.

Maybe it's a bird, I said, a big bird, resting. Birds grow tired, after they've flown over the country, up and down in the wind, looking down on all the sights, so sometimes, when they reach a tree, with good solid branches, they rest.

Silence

ELLEN

When I run . . . when I run . . . when I run . . . over the grass . . .

RUMSEY

She floats . . . under me. Floating . . . under me.

ELLEN

I turn. I turn. I wheel. I glide. I wheel. In stunning light. The horizon moves from the sun. I am crushed by the light.

Silence

RUMSEY

Sometimes I see people. They walk towards me, no, not so, walk in my direction, but never reaching me, turning left, or disappearing, and then reappearing, to disappear into the wood.

So many ways to lose sight of them, then to recapture sight of them. They are sharp at first sight . . . then smudged . . . then lost . . . then glimpsed again . . . then gone.

BATES

Funny. Sometimes I press my hand on my forehead, calmingly, feel all the dust drain out, let it go, feel the grit slip away. Funny moment. That calm moment.

ELLEN *moves to* RUMSEY

ELLEN

It's changed. You've painted it. You've made shelves. Everything. It's beautiful.

RUMSEY

Can you remember . . . when you were here last?

ELLEN

Oh yes.

RUMSEY

You were a little girl.

ELLEN

I was.

Pause

RUMSEY

Can you cook now?

ELLEN

Shall I cook for you?

RUMSEY

Yes.

ELLEN

Next time I come. I will.

Pause

                         RUMSEY

Do you like music?

                         ELLEN

Yes.

                         RUMSEY

I'll play you music.

Pause

                         RUMSEY

Look at your reflection.

                         ELLEN

Where?

                         RUMSEY

In the window.

                         ELLEN

It's very dark outside.

                         RUMSEY

It's high up.

                         ELLEN

Does it get darker the higher you get?

                         RUMSEY

No.

Silence

ELLEN

Around me sits the night. Such a silence. I can hear myself. Cup my ear. My heart beats in my ear. Such a silence. Is it me? Am I silent or speaking? How can I know? Can I know such things? No-one has ever told me. I need to be told things. I seem to be old. Am I old now? No-one will tell me. I must find a person to tell me these things.

BATES

My landlady asks me in for a drink. Stupid conversation. What are you doing here? Why do you live alone? Where do you come from? What do you do with yourself? What kind of life have you had? You seem fit. A bit grumpy. You can smile, surely, at something? Surely you have smiled, at a thing in your life? At something? Has there been no pleasantness in your life? No kind of loveliness in your life? Are you nothing but a childish old man, suffocating himself?

I've had all that. I've got all that. I said.

ELLEN

He sat me on his knee, by the window, and asked if he could kiss my right cheek. I nodded he could. He did. Then he asked, if, having kissed my right, he could do the same with my left. I said yes. He did.

Silence

RUMSEY

She was looking down. I couldn't hear what she said.

BATES

I can't hear you. Yes you can, I said.

RUMSEY

What are you saying? Look at me, she said.

BATES
I didn't. I didn't hear you, she said. I didn't hear what you said.

RUMSEY
But I am looking at you. It's your head that's bent.

Silence

BATES
The little girl looked up at me. I said: at night horses are quite happy. They stand about, then after a bit of a time they go to sleep. In the morning they wake up, snort a bit, canter, sometimes, and eat. You've no cause to worry about them.

ELLEN *moves to* RUMSEY

RUMSEY
Find a young man.

ELLEN
There aren't any.

RUMSEY
Don't be stupid.

ELLEN
I don't like them.

RUMSEY
You're stupid.

ELLEN

I hate them.

Pause

RUMSEY

Find one.

Silence

BATES

For instance, I said, those shapes in the trees, you'll find they're just birds, resting after a long journey.

ELLEN

I go up with the milk. The sky hits me. I walk in this wind to collide with them waiting.

There are two. They halt to laugh and bellow in the yard. They dig and punch and cackle where they stand. They turn to move, look round at me to grin. I turn my eyes from one, and from the other to him.

Silence

BATES

From the young people's room – silence. Sleep? Tender love?

It's of no importance.

Silence

RUMSEY

I walk with my girl who wears—

BATES

Caught a bus to the town. Crowds. Lights round—

Silence

ELLEN

After my work each day I walk back through people but I don't notice them. I'm not in a dream or anything of that sort. On the contrary. I'm quite wide awake to the world around me. But not to the people. There must be something in them to notice, to pay attention to, something of interest in them. In fact I know there is. I'm certain of it. But I pass through them noticing nothing. It is only later, in my room, that I remember. Yes, I remember. But I'm never sure that what I remember is of to-day or of yesterday or of a long time ago.

And then often it is only half things I remember, half things, beginnings of things.

My drinking companion for the hundredth time asked me if I'd ever been married. This time I told her I had. Yes, I told her I had. Certainly. I can remember the wedding.

Silence

RUMSEY

On good evenings we walk through the hills to the top of the hill past the dogs the clouds racing

ELLEN

Sometimes the wind is so high he does not hear me.

BATES

Brought her into this place, my cousin runs it.

ELLEN

all the blue changes, I'm dizzy sometimes

Silence

RUMSEY

that the path and the bushes are the same, that the gate is the same

BATES

You cross the field out of darkness.
You arrive.

ELLEN

I turn to them and speak.

Silence

RUMSEY

and watch the folding light.

BATES

and their tittering bitches, and their music, and their love.

ELLEN

They ask me where I come from. I say of course from the country.

Silence

BATES

Come with me tonight.

ELLEN

Where?

BATES

Anywhere. For a walk.

Silence

RUMSEY

My visit, my care, will be like any other visit, any other care.

BATES

I see something in a tree, a shape, a shadow.

Silence

ELLEN

When I run . . .

RUMSEY

Floating . . . under me.

ELLEN

The horizon moves from the sun.

Silence

RUMSEY

They are sharp at first sight . . . then smudged . . . then lost . . .
then glimpsed again . . . then gone.

BATES

feel all the dust drain out, let it go,

feel the grit slip away.

ELLEN

I look them in their eyes.

Silence

RUMSEY

It's high up.

ELLEN

Does it get darker the higher you get?

RUMSEY

No.

Silence

ELLEN

Around me sits the night. Such a silence.

BATES

I've had all that. I've got all that. I said.

ELLEN

I nodded he could.

Silence

RUMSEY

She was looking down.

BATES

Yes you can, I said.

RUMSEY

What are you saying?

BATES

I didn't hear you, she said.

RUMSEY

But I am looking at you. It's your head that's bent.

Silence

BATES

In the morning they wake up, snort a bit, canter, sometimes, and eat.

Silence

ELLEN

There aren't any.

RUMSEY

Don't be stupid.

ELLEN

I don't like them.

RUMSEY

You're stupid.

Silence

BATES

For instance, I said, those shapes in the trees.

ELLEN

I walk in this wind to collide with them waiting.

Silence

BATES

Sleep? Tender love? It's of no importance.

ELLEN

I kiss them there and say

Silence

RUMSEY

I walk

Silence

BATES

Caught a bus

Silence

ELLEN

Certainly. I can remember the wedding.

Silence

RUMSEY

I walk with my girl who wears a grey blouse

BATES

Caught a bus to the town. Crowds. Lights round the market

Long silence

Fade lights

Revue Sketches

NIGHT

THAT'S YOUR TROUBLE

THAT'S ALL

APPLICANT

INTERVIEW

DIALOGUE FOR THREE

NIGHT was first presented by Alexander H. Cohen Ltd in an entertainment entitled *Mixed Doubles* at the Comedy Theatre on 9th April, 1969, with the following cast:

MAN   Nigel Stock
WOMAN   Vivien Merchant
                Directed by Alexander Doré

THAT'S YOUR TROUBLE, THAT'S ALL, APPLICANT, INTERVIEW and DIALOGUE FOR THREE were first presented on B.B.C. Radio on the Third Programme between February and March 1964.

NIGHT

A woman and a man in their forties.
They sit with coffee.

MAN. I'm talking about that time by the river.
WOMAN. What time?
MAN. The first time. On the bridge. Starting on the bridge.

Pause.

WOMAN. I can't remember.
MAN. On the bridge. We stopped and looked down at the river.
It was night. There were lamps lit on the towpath. We were
alone. We looked up the river. I put my hand on the small
of your waist. Don't you remember? I put my hand under
your coat.

Pause.

WOMAN. Was it winter?
MAN. Of course it was winter. It was when we met. It was our
first walk. You must remember that.
WOMAN. I remember walking. I remember walking with you.
MAN. The first time? Our first walk?
WOMAN. Yes, of course, I remember that.

Pause.

We walked down a road into a field, through some railings.
We walked to a corner of the field and then we stood by the
railings.
MAN. No. It was on the bridge that we stopped.

Pause.

WOMAN. That was someone else.

MAN. Rubbish
WOMAN. That was another girl.
MAN. It was years ago. You've forgotten.

   Pause.

I remember the light on the water.
WOMAN. You took my face in your hands, standing by the railings. You were very gentle, you were very caring. You cared. Your eyes searched my face. I wondered who you were. I wondered what you thought. I wondered what you would do.
MAN. You agree we met at a party. You agree with that?
WOMAN. What was that?
MAN. What?
WOMAN. I thought I heard a child crying.
MAN. There was no sound.
WOMAN. I thought it was a child, crying, waking up.
MAN. The house is silent.

   Pause.

It's very late. We're sitting here. We should be in bed. I have to be up early. I have things to do. Why do you argue?
WOMAN. I don't. I'm not. I'm willing to go to bed. I have things to do. I have to be up in the morning.

   Pause.

MAN. A man called Doughty gave the party. You knew him. I had met him. I knew his wife. I met you there. You were standing by the window. I smiled at you, and to my surprise you smiled back. You liked me. I was amazed. You found me attractive. Later you told me. You liked my eyes.
WOMAN. You liked mine.

   Pause.

You touched my hand. You asked me who I was, and what

I was, and whether I was aware that you were touching my hand, that your fingers were touching mine, that your fingers were moving up and down between mine.

MAN. No. We stopped on a bridge. I stood behind you. I put my hand under your coat, onto your waist. You felt my hand on you.

Pause.

WOMAN. We had been to a party. Given by the Doughtys. You had known his wife. She looked at you dearly, as if to say you were her dear. She seemed to love you. I didn't. I didn't know you. They had a lovely house. By a river. I went to collect my coat, leaving you waiting for me. You had offered to escort me. I thought you were quite courtly, quite courteous, pleasantly mannered, quite caring. I slipped my coat on and looked out of the window, knowing you were waiting. I looked down over the garden to the river, and saw the lamplight on the water. Then I joined you and we walked down the road through railings into a field, must have been some kind of park. Later we found your car. You drove me.

Pause.

MAN. I touched your breasts.
WOMAN. Where?
MAN. On the bridge. I felt your breasts.
WOMAN. Really?
MAN. Standing behind you.
WOMAN. I wondered whether you would, whether you wanted to, whether you would.
MAN. Yes.
WOMAN. I wondered how you would go about it, whether you wanted to, sufficiently.
MAN. I put my hands under your sweater, I undid your brassière, I felt your breasts.
WOMAN. Another night perhaps. Another girl.

MAN. You don't remember my fingers on your skin?

WOMAN. Were they in your hands? My breasts? Fully in your hands?

MAN. You don't remember my hands on your skin?

Pause.

WOMAN. Standing behind me?

MAN. Yes.

WOMAN. But my back was against railings. I felt the railings .. behind me. You were facing me. I was looking into your eyes. My coat was closed. It was cold.

MAN. I undid your coat.

WOMAN. It was very late. Chilly.

MAN. And then we left the bridge and we walked down the towpath and we came to a rubbish dump.

WOMAN. And you had me and you told me you had fallen in love with me, and you said you would take care of me always, and you told me my voice and my eyes, my thighs, my breasts, were incomparable, and that you would adore me always.

MAN. Yes I did.

WOMAN. And you do adore me always.

MAN. Yes I do.

WOMAN. And then we had children and we sat and talked and you remembered women on bridges and towpaths and rubbish dumps.

MAN. And you remembered your bottom against railings and men holding your hands and men looking into your eyes.

WOMAN. And talking to me softly.

MAN. And your soft voice. Talking to them softly at night.

WOMAN. And they said I will adore you always.

MAN. Saying I will adore you always.

THAT'S YOUR TROUBLE

Two men in a park. One on the grass, reading. The other making cricket strokes with umbrella.

1. A. (*stopping in mid-stroke*): Eh, look at that bloke, what s he got on his back, he's got a sandwich board on his back.
2. B.: What about it?
3. A.: He wants to take it off, he'll get a headache.
4. B.: Rubbish.
5. A.: What do you mean?
6. B.: He won't get a headache.
7. A.: I bet he will.
8. B.: The neck! It affects his neck! He'll get a neckache.
9. A.: The strain goes up.
10. B.: Have you ever carried a sandwich board?
11. A.: Never.
12. B.: Then how do you know which way the strain *goes*? (*Pause.*) It goes down! The strain goes down, it starts with the neck and it goes down. He'll get a neckache and a backache.
13. A.: He'll get a headache in the end.
14. B.: There's no end.
15. A.: That's where the brain is.
16. B.: That's where the *what* is?
17. A.: The brain.
18. B.: It's nothing to do with the brain.
19. A.: Oh, isn't it?
20. B.: It won't go anywhere *near* his brain.
21. A.: That's where you're wrong.
22. B.: I'm not wrong. I'm right. (*Pause.*) You happen to be talking to a man who knows what he's talking about. (*Pause.*) His brain doesn't come into it. If you've got a strain, it goes down. It's not like heat.

23. A.: What do you mean?
24. B. (*ferociously*): If you've got a strain it goes down! Heat goes up! (*Pause.*)
25. A.: You mean sound.
26. B.: I what?
27. A.: Sound goes up.
28. B.: Sound goes anywhere it likes! It all depends where you happen to be standing, it's a matter of physics, that's something you're just completely ignorant of, but you just try carrying a sandwich board and you'll find out soon enough. First the neck, than the shoulders, then the back, then it worms into the buttocks, that's where it worms. The buttocks. Either the right or the left, it depends how you carry your weight. Then right down the thighs – a straight drop to his feet and he'll collapse.
29. A.: He hasn't collapsed yet.
30. B.: He will. Give him a chance. A headache! How can he get a headache? He hasn't got anything on his head! I'm the one who's got the headache. (*Pause.*) You just don't know how to listen to what other people tell you, that's your trouble.
31. A.: I know what my trouble is.
32. B.: You don't know what your trouble is, my friend. That's your trouble.

THAT'S ALL

MRS. A.: I always put the kettle on about that time.

MRS. B.: Yes. (*Pause.*)

MRS. A.: Then she comes round.

MRS. B.: Yes. (*Pause.*)

MRS. A.: Only on Thursdays.

MRS. B.: Yes. (*Pause.*)

MRS. A.: On Wednesdays I used to put it on. When she used to come round. Then she changed it to Thursdays.

MRS. B.: Oh yes.

MRS. A.: After she moved. When she used to live round the corner, then she always came in on Wednesdays, but then when she moved she used to come down to the butcher's on Thursdays. She couldn't find a butcher up there.

MRS. B.: No.

MRS. A.: Anyway, she decided she'd stick to her own butcher. Well, I thought, if she can't find a butcher, that's the best thing.

MRS. B.: Yes. (*Pause.*)

MRS. A.: So she started to come down on Thursdays. I didn't know she was coming down on Thursdays until one day I met her in the butcher.

MRS. B.: Oh yes.

MRS. A.: It wasn't my day for the butcher, I don't go to the butcher on Thursdays.

MRS. B.: No, I know. (*Pause.*)

MRS. A.: I go on Friday.

MRS. B.: Yes. (*Pause.*)

MRS. A.: That's where I see you.

MRS. B.: Yes. (*Pause.*)

MRS. A.: You're always in there on Fridays.

MRS. B.: Oh yes. (*Pause.*)

MRS. A.: But I happened to go in for a bit of meat, it turned out to be a Thursday. I wasn't going in for my usual weekly on Friday. I just slipped in, the day before.

MRS. B.: Yes.

MRS. A.: That was the first time I found out she couldn't find a butcher up there, so she decided to come back here, once a week, to her own butcher.

MRS. B.: Yes.

MRS. A.: She came on Thursday so she'd be able to get meat for the weekend. Lasted her till Monday, then from Monday to Thursday they'd have fish. She can always buy cold meat, if they want a change.

MRS. B.: Oh yes. (*Pause.*)

MRS. A.: So I told her to come in when she came down after she'd been to the butcher's and I'd put a kettle on. So she did. (*Pause.*)

MRS. B.: Yes. (*Pause.*)

MRS. A.: It was funny because she always used to come in Wednesdays. (*Pause.*) Still, it made a break. (*Long pause.*)

MRS. B.: She doesn't come in no more, does she? (*Pause.*)

MRS. A.: She comes in. She doesn't come in so much, but she comes in. (*Pause.*)

MRS. B.: I thought she didn't come in. (*Pause.*)

MRS. A.: She comes in. (*Pause.*) She just doesn't come in so much. That's all.

APPLICANT

An office, LAMB, *a young man, eager, cheerful, enthusiastic, is striding nervously, alone. The door opens.* MISS PIFFS *comes in. She is the essence of efficiency.*

PIFFS: Ah, good morning.

LAMB: Oh, good morning, miss.

PIFFS: Are you Mr. Lamb?

LAMB: That's right.

PIFFS [*studying a sheet of paper*]: Yes, You're applying for this vacant post, aren't you?

LAMB: I am actually, yes.

PIFFS: Are you a physicist?

LAMB: Oh yes, indeed. It's my whole life.

PIFFS [*languidly*]: Good. Now our procedure is, that before we discuss the applicant's qualifications we like to subject him to a little test to determine his psychological suitability. You've no objection?

LAMB: Oh, good heavens, no.

PIFFS: Jolly good.

> MISS PIFFS *has taken some objects out of a drawer and goes to* LAMB. *She places a chair for him.*

PIFFS: Please sit down. [*He sits.*] Can I fit these to your palms?

LAMB [*affably*]: What are they?

PIFFS: Electrodes.

LAMB: Oh yes, of course. Funny little things.

> *She attaches them to his palms.*

PIFFS: Now the earphones.

> *She attaches earphones to his head.*

LAMB: I say how amusing.
PIFFS: Now I plug in.

She plugs in to the wall.

LAMB [*a trifle nervously*]: Plug in, do you? Oh yes, of course.
Yes, you'd have to, wouldn't you?

MISS PIFFS *perches on a high stool and looks down on*
LAMB.

This help to determine my . . . my suitability does it?
PIFFS: Unquestionably. Now relax. Just relax. Don't think
about a thing.
LAMB: No.
PIFFS: Relax completely. Rela-a-a-x. Quite relaxed?

LAMB *nods.* MISS PIFFS *presses a button on the side of her
stool. A piercing high pitched buzz-hum is heard.* LAMB *jolts
rigid. His hands go to his earphones. He is propelled from the
chair. He tries to crawl under the chair.* MISS PIFFS
watches, impassive. The noise stops. LAMB *peeps out from
under the chair, crawls out, stands, twitches, emits a short
chuckle and collapses in the chair.*

PIFFS: Would you say you were an excitable person?
LAMB: Not – not unduly, no. Of course, I—
PIFFS: Would you say you were a moody person?
LAMB: Moody? No, I wouldn't say I was moody – well,
sometimes occasionally I—
PIFFS: Do you ever get fits of depression?
LAMB: Well, I wouldn't call them depression exactly—
PIFFS: Do you often do things you regret in the morning?
LAMB: Regret? Things I regret? Well, it depends what you
mean by often, really – I mean when you say often—
PIFFS: Are you often puzzled by women?
LAMB: Women?
PIFFS: Men.

LAMB: Men? Well, I was just going to answer the question about women—
PIFFS: Do you often feel puzzled?
LAMB: Puzzled?
PIFFS: By women.
LAMB: Women?
PIFFS: Men.
LAMB: Oh, now just a minute, I ... Look, do you want separate answers or a joint answer?
PIFFS: After your day's work do you ever feel tired? Edgy? Fretty? Irritable? At a loose end? Morose? Frustrated? Morbid? Unable to concentrate? Unable to sleep? Unable to eat? Unable to remain seated? Unable to remain upright? Lustful? Indolent? On heat? Randy? Full of desire? Full of energy? Full of dread? Drained? of energy, of dread? of desire?

   Pause.

LAMB [*thinking*]: Well, it's difficult to say really ...
PIFFS: Are you a good mixer?
LAMB: Well, you've touched on quite an interesting point there—
PIFFS: Do you suffer from eczema, listlessness, or falling coat?
LAMB: Er ...
PIFFS: Are you virgo intacta?
LAMB: I beg your pardon?
PIFFS: Are you virgo intacta?
LAMB: Oh, I say, that's rather embarrassing. I mean – in front of a lady—
PIFFS: Are you virgo intacta?
LAMB: Yes, I am, actually. I'll make no secret of it.
PIFFS: Have you always been virgo intacta?
LAMB: Oh yes, always. Always.
PIFFS: From the word go?
LAMB: Go? Oh yes, from the word go.

PIFFS: Do women frighten you?

She presses a button on the other side of her stool. The stage is plunged into redness, which flashes on and off in time with her questions.

PIFFS [*building*]: Their clothes? Their shoes? Their voices? Their laughter? Their stares? Their way of walking? Their way of sitting? Their way of smiling? Their way of talking? Their mouths? Their hands? Their feet? Their shins? Their thighs? Their knees? Their eyes?
Their [*Drumbeat*]. Their [*Drumbeat*]. Their [*Cymbal bang*]. Their [*Trombone chord*]. Their [*Bass note*].

LAMB [*in a high voice*]: Well it depends what you mean really—

The light still flashes. She presses the other button and the piercing buzz-hum is heard again. LAMB's *hands go to his earphones. He is propelled from the chair, falls, rolls, crawls, totters and collapses.*

Silence.

He lies face upwards. MISS PIFFS *looks at him then walks to* LAMB *and bends over him.*

PIFFS: Thank you very much, Mr. Lamb. We'll let you know.

INTERVIEW

INTERVIEWER: Well, Mr. Jakes, how would you say things are in the pornographic book trade?

JAKES: I make 200 a week.

INTERVIEWER: 200?

JAKES: Yes, I make round about 200 a week at it.

INTERVIEWER: I see. So how would you say things were in the pornographic book trade?

JAKES: Oh, only fair.

INTERVIEWER: Only fair?

JAKES: Fair to middling.

INTERVIEWER: Why would you say that, Mr. Jakes?

JAKES: Well, it's got a lot to do with Xmas, between you and me.

INTERVIEWER: Xmas?

JAKES: Yes, well what happens is, you see, is that the trade takes a bit of a bashing round about Xmas time. Takes a good few months to recover from Xmas time, the pornographic book trade does.

INTERVIEWER: Oh, I see.

JAKES: Yes, what's got something to do with it is, you see, that you don't get all that many people sending pornographic books for Xmas presents. I mean, you get a few, of course, but not all that many. No, we can't really say that people in our trade get much benefit from the Xmas spirit, if you know what I mean.

INTERVIEWER: Well, I'm sorry to hear that, Mr. Jakes.

JAKES: Well, there you are. We make the best of it. (*Pause.*) I mean I put a sprig of holly . . . here and there . . . I put holly up all over the shop, but it doesn't seem to make much difference. (*Pause.*)

INTERVIEWER: What sort of people do you get in your shop, Mr. Jakes?

JAKES: I beg your pardon?

INTERVIEWER: What sort of people do you get in your shop?

JAKES: I'd rather not answer that question, thanks.

INTERVIEWER: Why not?

JAKES: I should think the security police could tell you a thing or two about that.

INTERVIEWER: Security police?

JAKES: Yes. They've got their dossiers, don't you worry about that.

INTERVIEWER: But we have no security police in this country.

JAKES: Don't you? You'd be surprised. They know all about it, take it from me. I've seen their dossiers.

INTERVIEWER: You've seen their dossiers?

JAKES: Dossiers? I've looked at more of their dossiers than you've had nights off.

INTERVIEWER: I see. Well, perhaps we'd better pass on to another question.

JAKES: Dossiers? I've been there morning and afternoon checking over their dossiers, identifying my customers, identifying their photographs right into the middle of the night, right into the middle of their dossiers.

INTERVIEWER: I had no idea—

JAKES: We've got them all taped in the pornographic book trade, don't you worry about that.

INTERVIEWER: Yes, well—

JAKES: You've no need to become anxious about *that*.

INTERVIEWER: Mr Jakes—

JAKES: Every single individual that passes through my door goes out.

INTERVIEWER: What?

JAKES: Every single dirty-minded individual that passes through my door goes straight out again. As soon as he's chosen his fancy – out he goes.

INTERVIEWER: You don't . . . keep them in?

JAKES: Keep them in! Never! I wouldn't keep one of them

in my own little pornographic bookshop, not me. Not that they haven't begged, mind you. Begged. They've gone down on their bended knees and begged me to allow them to stay the night in the backroom, in the punishment section. Not me. Not since I got the word.

INTERVIEWER: I think perhaps—

JAKES (*confidentially*): You don't think the security police are the only people who've got dossiers, do you?

INTERVIEWER: No, I'm sure—

JAKES: You don't think that, do you? Get out of it. I'm up half the night doing my dossiers! I've got one on every single member of my clientele. And the day's coming, my boy, I can tell you.

INTERVIEWER: Coming?

JAKES: We're going to hold a special exhibition, see? We'll have them all in there, white in the face, peeping, peering, sweating, showing me false credentials to get to the top shelf, and then at a given moment we lock the doors and turn the floodlights on. And then we'll have them all revealed for what they are.

INTERVIEWER: What . . . are they?

JAKES: They're all the same, every single one of them. COMMUNISTS.

DIALOGUE FOR THREE

IST MAN: Did I ever tell you about the woman in the blue dress? I met her in Casablanca. She was a spy. A spy in a blue dress. That woman was an agent for another power. She was tattooed on her belly with a pelican. Her belly was covered with a pelican. She could make that pelican waddle across the room to you. On all fours, sideways, feet first, arseupwards, any way you like. Her control was superhuman. Only a woman could possess it. Under her blue dress she wore a shimmy. And under her shimmy she wore a pelican.

2ND MAN: The snow has turned to slush.

IST MAN: The temperature must have dropped.

WOMAN: Sometimes I think I'm not feminine enough for you.

IST MAN: You are.

WOMAN: Or do you think I should be more feminine?

IST MAN: No.

WOMAN: Perhaps I should be more masculine.

IST MAN: Certainly not.

WOMAN: You think I'm too feminine?

IST MAN: No.

WOMAN: If I didn't love you so much it wouldn't matter. Do you remember the first time we met? On the beach? In the night? All those people? And the bonfire? And the waves? And the spray? And the mist? And the moon? Everyone dancing, somersaulting, laughing? And you – standing silent, staring at a sandcastle in your sheer white trunks. The moon was behind you, in front of you, all over you, suffusing you, consuming you, you were transparent, translucent, a beacon. I was struck dumb, dumbstruck. Water rose up my legs. I could not move. I was rigid. Immovable. Our eyes met. Love at first sight. I held your gaze. And in your eyes, bold and unashamed, was desire. Brutal, demanding desire. Bestial, ruthless, remorseless. I stood there magnetised, hypnotised. Transfixed. Motionless and still. A spider caught in a web.

1ST MAN (*to* 2ND MAN): You know who you remind me of? You remind me of Whipper Wallace, back in the good old days. He used to knock about with a chap called House Peters. Boghouse Peters we used to call him. I remember one day Whipper and Boghouse – he had a scar on his left cheek, Boghouse, caught in some boghouse brawl, I suppose – well, anyway, there they were, the Whipper and Boghouse, rolling down by the banks of the Euphrates this night, when up came a policeman ...... up came this policeman ...... up came a policeman ...... this policeman ...... approached ...... Boghouse ...... and the Whipper ...... were questioned ...... this night ...... the Euphrates ...... a policeman ......

Tea Party

(Short Story)

*I wrote this short story in 1963, and in 1964 was commissioned by
the B.B.C. to write a play for the European Broadcasting Union.
I decided to treat the same subject in play form. In my view, the
story is the more successful.*

H.P.

My eyes are worse.

My physician is an inch under six feet. There is a grey strip in his hair, one, no more. He has a brown stain on his left cheek. His lampshades are dark blue drums. Each has a golden rim. They are identical. There is a deep black burn in his Indian carpet. His staff is bespectacled, to a woman. Through the blinds I hear the birds of his garden. Sometimes his wife appears, in white.

He is clearly sceptical on the subject of my eyes. According to him my eyes are normal, perhaps even better than normal. He finds no evidence that my sight is growing worse.

My eyes are worse. It is not that I do not see. I do see.

My job goes well. My family and I remain close friends. My two sons are my closest friends. My wife is closer. I am close friends with all my family, including my mother and my father. Often we sit and listen to Bach. When I go to Scotland I take them with me. My wife's brother came once, and was useful on the trip.

I have my hobbies, one of which is using a hammer and nails, or a screwdriver and screws, or various saws, on wood, constructing things or making things useful, finding a use for an object which appears to have no value. But it is not so easy to do this when you see double, or when you are blinded by the object, or when you do not see at all, or when you are blinded by the object.

My wife is happy. I use my imagination in bed. We love with the light on. I watch her closely, she watches me. In the

morning her eyes shine. I can see them shining through her
spectacles.

All winter the skies were bright. Rain fell at night. In the morning the skies were bright. My backhand flip was my strongest
weapon. Taking position to face my wife's brother, across the
dear table, my bat lightly clasped, my wrist flexing, I waited to
loosen my flip to his forehand, watch him (*shocked*) dart and be
beaten, flounder and sulk. My forehand was not so powerful, so
swift. Predictably, he attacked my forehand. There was a
ringing sound in the room, a rubber sound in the walls. Predictably, he attacked my forehand. But once far to the right on
my forehand, and my weight genuinely disposed, I could
employ my backhand flip, unanswerable, watch him flounder,
skid and be beaten. They were close games. But it is not now so
easy when you see the pingpong ball double, or do not see it at
all or when, hurtling towards you at speed, the ball blinds you.

I am pleased with my secretary. She knows the business well
and loves it. She is trustworthy. She makes calls to Newcastle
and Birmingham on my behalf and is never fobbed off. She is
respected on the telephone. Her voice is persuasive. My partner
and I agree that she is of inestimable value to us. My partner
and my wife often discuss her when the three of us meet for
coffee or drinks. Neither of them, when discussing Wendy,
can speak highly enough of her.

On bright days, of which there are many, I pull the blinds in
my office in order to dictate. Often I touch her swelling body.
She reads back, flips the page. She makes a telephone call to
Birmingham. Even were I, while she speaks (holding the re-
ceiver lightly, her other hand poised for notes), to touch her
swelling body, her call would still be followed to its conclusion.
It is she who bandages my eyes, while I touch her swelling
body.

I do not remember being like my sons in any way when I was a boy. Their reserve is remarkable. They seem stirred by no passion. They sit silent. An odd mutter passes between them. I can't hear you, what are you saying, speak up, I say. My wife says the same. I can't hear you, what are you saying, speak up. They are of an age. They work well at school, it appears. But at pingpong both are duds. As a boy I was wide awake, of passionate interests, voluble, responsive, and my eyesight was excellent. They resemble me in no way. Their eyes are glazed and evasive behind their spectacles.

My brother in law was best man at our wedding. None of my friends were at that time in the country. My closest friend, who was the natural choice, was called away suddenly on business. To his great regret, he was therefore forced to opt out. He had prepared a superb speech in honour of the groom, to be delivered at the reception. My brother in law could not of course himself deliver it, since it referred to the longstanding friendship which existed between Atkins and myself, and my brother in law knew little of me. He was therefore confronted with a difficult problem. He solved it by making his sister his central point of reference. I still have the present he gave me, a carved pencil sharpener, from Bali.

The day I first interviewed Wendy she wore a tight tweed skirt. Her left thigh never ceased to caress her right, and vice versa. All this took place under her skirt. She seemed to me the perfect secretary. She listened to my counsel wide-eyed and attentive, her hands calmly clasped, trim, bulgy, plump, rosy, swelling. She was clearly the possessor of an active and inquiring intelligence. Three times she cleaned her spectacles with a silken kerchief.

After the wedding my brother in law asked my dear wife to remove her glasses. He peered deep into her eyes. You have married a good man, he said. He will make you happy. As he was doing nothing at the time I invited him to join me in the business. Before long he became my partner, so keen was his industry, so sharp his business acumen.

Wendy's commonsense, her clarity, her discretion, are of inestimable value to our firm.

With my eye at the keyhole I hear goosing, the squeak of them. The slit is black, only the sliding gussle on my drum, the hiss and flap of their bliss. The room sits on my head, my skull creased on the brass and loathsome handle I dare not twist, for fear of seeing black screech and scrape of my secretary writhing blind in my partner's paunch and jungle.

My wife reached down to me. Do you love me, she asked. I do love you, I spat into her eyeball. I shall prove it yet, I shall prove it yet, what proof yet, what proof remaining, what proof not yet given. All proof. (For my part, I decided on a more cunning, more allusive strategem.) Do you love me, was my counter.

The pingpong table streaked with slime. My hands pant to gain the ball. My sons watch. They cheer me on. They are loud in their loyalty. I am moved. I fall back on strokes, on gambits, long since gone, flip, cut, chop, shtip, bluff to my uttermost. I play the ball by nose. The twins hail my efforts gustily. But my brother in law is no chump. He slams again, he slams again, deep to my forehand. I skid, flounder, stare sightless into the crack of his bat.

Where are my hammers, my screws, my saws?

How are you? asked my partner. Bandage on straight? Knots tight?

The door slammed. Where was I? In the office or at home? Had someone come in as my partner went out? Had he gone out? Was it silence I heard, this scuffle, creak, squeal, scrape, gurgle and muff? Tea was being poured. Heavy thighs (Wendy's? my wife's? both? apart? together?) trembled in stilletos. I sipped the liquid. It was welcome. My physician greeted me warmly. In a minute, old chap, we'll take off those bandages. Have a rock cake. I declined. The birds are at the bird bath, called his white wife. They all rushed to look. My sons sent something flying. *Someone?* Surely not. I had never heard my sons in such good form. They chattered, chuckled, discussed their work eagerly with their uncle. My parents were silent. The room seemed very small, smaller than I had remembered it. I knew where everything was, every particular. But its smell had altered. Perhaps because the room was overcrowded. My wife broke gasping out of a fit of laughter, as she was wont to do in the early days of our marriage. Why was she laughing? Had someone told her a joke? Who? Her sons? Unlikely. My sons were discussing their work with my physician and his wife. Be with you in a minute, old chap, my physician called to me. Meanwhile my partner had the two women half stripped on a convenient rostrum. Whose body swelled most? I had forgotten. I picked up a pingpong ball. It was hard. I wondered how far he had stripped the women. The top halves or the bottom halves? Or perhaps he was now raising his spectacles to view my wife's swelling buttocks, the swelling breasts of my secretary. How could I verify this? By movement, by touch. But that was out of the question. And could such a sight possibly take place under the eyes of my own children? Would they continue to chat and chuckle, as they still did, with my physician? Hardly. However, it was good to have the bandage on straight and the knots tight.

DATE DUE
